Financial Success

Money basics that all young people should know, but don't

By David Matheson & Tammy Prestage

ABOUT THIS COURSE

This course is designed to equip students with essential financial knowledge and practical skills to navigate real-world financial responsibilities with confidence. Aligned with the values of Southern Cross Catholic College, the program empowers students to make informed, ethical, and sustainable financial decisions as they transition into adulthood.

ABOUT SOUTHERN CROSS ACADEMY

Southern Cross Catholic College in Burwood is an award-winning, dynamic coeducational Year 10–12 college, nationally recognised for its innovation and forward-thinking approach to senior secondary education. The College blends vocational education and training (VET) and Higher School Certificate pathways seamlessly, offering dual qualifications, apprenticeships, traineeships, and more than 30 vocational courses. Bespoke programs such as the pioneering Year 10 Financial Success course reflect a commitment to advanced, practical, hands-on learning designed by leading educators and industry experts. Flexible timetables, industry-standard state-of-the-art facilities, and extensive workplace immersion, ensure students graduate confident, capable, and work-ready. Guided by its motto Head, Heart, and Hands, Southern Cross empowers every learner to achieve success, aspiring to personal excellence in a supportive, faith-filled community.

ACKNOWLEDGEMENTS

Grateful thanks are extended to Allanah Vom Bruch for her contribution to research and content in this book and to Melinda Holme for her graphic design and layout, which have brought this text to life.

ABOUT THE AUTHORS

David Matheson

David joined Southern Cross in 2025 as Assistant Principal, bringing over 20 years of educational leadership experience from Independent and Systemic Schools across greater Sydney. His diverse expertise spans curriculum, wellbeing, operational, and faith leadership domains. Holding Master's degrees in Educational Leadership and Religious Education, David is committed to relational leadership, fostering high expectations, and leveraging technology for emerging youth opportunities.

Tammy Prestage

A dynamic and visionary educator, Tammy brings over 30 years of experience to her role as Principal, joining Southern Cross Catholic College in 2023. With a distinguished background in vocational education and pathways innovation, she believes in the power of education to transform lives. She is committed to developing bespoke programs and opportunities that recognise each learner's strengths and aspirations, shaping a vibrant and inclusive community where every student can grow, thrive, and experience success.

Throughout this book you will find a range of links to further information. All of those links are available through the support website found at the following URL.

https://sites.google.com/syd.catholic.edu.au/southern-cross-academy/financial-success

SCAN FOR SUPPORT LINKS

Literature Review and Course Rationale

Financial literacy is increasingly recognised as a critical life skill, especially for young people navigating a rapidly changing economic landscape, where the range and complexity of financial products and services continue to expand. While from a consumer choice perspective, advancements in service offerings provide benefits to users, it is imperative that individuals engaging with these services have an adequate understanding.

Financial literacy, described by the Reserve Bank of Australia (RBA) as "a set of skills that allow people to manage their money wisely" (Hall, 2008, p. 12), is vital to empower individuals to take full advantage of financial products and services available. Hall, in his Address to the Conference on Deepening Financial Capacity in the Pacific Region, has drawn connections to those who make poor financial decisions, ending up with a lower standard of living than was otherwise achievable (2008). The fourth most common regret surrounding finances, as reported by Australians in The Future of Personal Finance in Australia report, was 'not learning more about finances and money', and most participants strongly supported the notion of implementing financial capability training in high schools (Breidbach et al., 2019a). In 2018, the Australian Securities and Investments Commission (ASIC) reported that one in three people finds dealing with money stressful and overwhelming, and in turn, the National Financial Literacy Strategy 2018 set the first priority to "educate the next generation, particularly through the formal education system" (Australian Government, 2018).

Young Australians are managing money day to day as active consumers, and between the ages of 13-17, while still school students, many are experiencing significant financial firsts, which may include first employment, filing tax returns, and utilising debit cards (Moneysmart, 2021). While young Australians are starting to use financial services, this group has been identified as having low financial literacy (de Zwaan & West). A study by de Zwaan and West (2022) found that while some students were familiar with basic financial terms, most lacked a deeper understanding of personal finance concepts such as interest, superannuation, and budgeting. Predominantly, students recall learning about money and financial concepts at home, with some also recalling topics explored in school in discipline areas such as Mathematics or Business Studies (de Zwaan & West, p. 2). However, these areas being the only touchpoints for financial literacy leads to students having inconsistent and often inadequate financial knowledge. While financial literacy is embedded in the Australian Curriculum through subjects such as Mathematics and Economics and Business, its coverage is often fragmented and lacks consistency across schools and states. The Financial Literacy of Young Australians report by de Zwaan and West highlights that many students do not find Mathematics an effective context for learning about money, and that Business Studies students tend to be more financially informed than their peers. This underscores the need for a dedicated, accessible course that complements the existing curriculum and reaches all students, regardless of subject selection.

With financial literacy having a direct impact on standards of living, it is recommended that financial literacy programs should be elevated within high schools, ideally as a stand-alone program (de Zwaan & West, p. 3). Financial concern was determined to be the number one concern for young people in Australia, with it being listed as the second biggest concern (after climate change) for older Australians (Real Insurance, as cited in Breidbach et al., 2019b). Despite this, in the Household, Income and Labour Dynamics in Australia (HILDA) survey of 2022, indications show that Australians' average financial literacy scores are declining (Hall, 2024), demonstrating the need for more proactive and early intervention programs.

In the 2021 ASIC Young People and Money survey, young people expressed a desire to gain further knowledge on a variety of money topics, including saving money, investing, filing a tax return, managing money, setting financial goals such as buying a car or property, and achieving them

(Moneysmart, 2021, p. 15). In de Zwaan and West's survey, over 50% of those surveyed stated they would benefit from formal education on the following:

- Taxes
- Investing
- Loans and debt
- Budgeting
- Life Insurance
- Superannuation
- Running a business
- Interest Rates
- Buying a car
- Saving

In addition to identifying the areas in which students seek further education and training, the mode of delivery and course design are critical to achieving meaningful learning outcomes. Findings from de Zwaan and West's study indicate that students demonstrated a relatively advanced understanding of financial concepts when these were contextualised through relatable narratives. This highlights the importance of embedding financial literacy within authentic, story-based learning experiences. Assessment design should also reflect this approach, as existing literature notes that many individuals struggle with understanding percentages (Lusardi, 2012, as cited in de Zwaan & West, 2022). Consequently, activities that rely solely on numerical calculations may risk disengaging some learners, underscoring the need for diverse, accessible, and contextually grounded assessment strategies.

An integrated, school-based financial literacy module, designed to align with curriculum outcomes, supported by technology, and informed by student voice, offers a powerful solution to a well-documented area of concern. By embedding financial education within the broader learning journey and grounding it in the values of the school community, a program of this nature can foster not only financial competence but also ethical decision-making, confidence, and well-being. With mechanisms in place for ongoing review, student feedback, and leadership oversight, this model ensures responsiveness to evolving needs and the flexibility to grow in scope and impact. Ultimately, equipping students with the knowledge and skills to navigate their financial futures is not just an educational imperative; it is a vital investment in their lifelong well-being and in the economic resilience of our broader society.

The following learning outcomes are mapped throughout this text and align with the Australian and NSW Curriculum.

LEARNING OUTCOME	DESCRIPTION	AUSTRALIAN CURRICULUM (9) CONTENT DESCRIPTORS	NSW CURRICULUM
LO1	Demonstrate personal financial management skills by applying knowledge of budgeting, saving, earning, and spending to real-world scenarios.	AC9M9N01: Recognise that the real number system includes the rational numbers and the irrational numbers, and solve problems involving real numbers using digital tools. AC9M9A05: Use Mathematical modelling to solve applied problems involving change, including financial contexts. AC9HE10K03: Factors that influence major consumer and financial decisions, and the short- and long-term consequences of these decisions.	MA5-FIN-C-01: Solves financial problems involving simple interest, earning money, and spending money. MA5-FIN-C-02: Solves financial problems involving compound interest and depreciation. CO5-FIN-01: Applies strategies to manage financial risks and rewards in the current financial landscape.
LO2	Analyse and evaluate financial products and services using critical thinking and cost-benefit analysis to make informed decisions.	AC9HE9K01: The role of Australia's financial sector and its effect on economic decision-making by individuals, businesses, and global markets. AC9HE10K04: The importance of Australia's superannuation system and how this system affects consumer and financial decision-making. AC9HE10S04: Develop and evaluate a response to an economic and business issue, using cost-benefit analysis or criteria to decide on a course of action.	CO5-ECB-01: Explains economic and business concepts and processes. CO5-FIN-01: Applies strategies to manage financial risks and rewards in the current financial landscape.
LO3	Understand and exercise roles, rights, and responsibilities as consumers in both physical and digital environments.	AC9HE9K05: How individuals and businesses manage consumer and financial risks and rewards. AC9TDI10P13: Develop cybersecurity threat models, and explore a software, user, or software supply chain vulnerability. AC9TDI10P14: Apply the Australian Privacy Principles to critique and manage the digital footprint that existing systems and student solutions collect.	COLS-RRI-01: Identifies the rights and responsibilities of individuals. COLS-SAF-01: Demonstrates safe practices in using a range of online processes.
LO4	Communicate financial ideas and decisions effectively using appropriate terminology, digital tools, and data representations.	AC9HE10S05: Create descriptions, explanations, and arguments, using economic and business knowledge, concepts, and terms that incorporate and acknowledge research findings. AC9M10ST03: Construct scatterplots and comment on the association between the two numerical variables in terms of strength, direction, and linearity. AC9HE9S05: Create descriptions, explanations, and arguments, using economic and business knowledge, concepts, and terms that incorporate and acknowledge research findings.	CO5-ECB-01: Explains economic and business concepts and processes. MA5.2-12SP: Uses statistical displays to interpret data.
LO5	Reflect on the ethical and social implications of financial decisions, considering the impact on self, community, and the environment.	AC9HE9K05: How individuals and businesses manage consumer and financial risks and rewards. AC9HE10K02: The ways that the government intervenes in the economy to improve economic performance and living standards within Australian society. AC9HG10K04: Causes and effects of a change in an identified environment at a local, national, or global scale, and strategies to manage sustainability.	CO5-FIN-01: Applies strategies to manage financial risks and rewards in the current financial landscape. CO5-ECB-01: Explains economic and business concepts and processes. COLS-FIN-01: Demonstrates financial literacy skills.

In addition to the mapped curriculum outcomes the following content descriptors from the Year 9 – 10 Australian Curriculum are addressed within this package.

It is acknowledged that the Australian Curriculum website further elaborates on each of the following descriptors https://www.australiancurriculum.edu.au/content/dam/en/curriculum/ac-version-9/curriculum-connections/consumer-and-financial-literacy/Consumer-and-financial-literacy-mapping-Year-9-and-10.docx

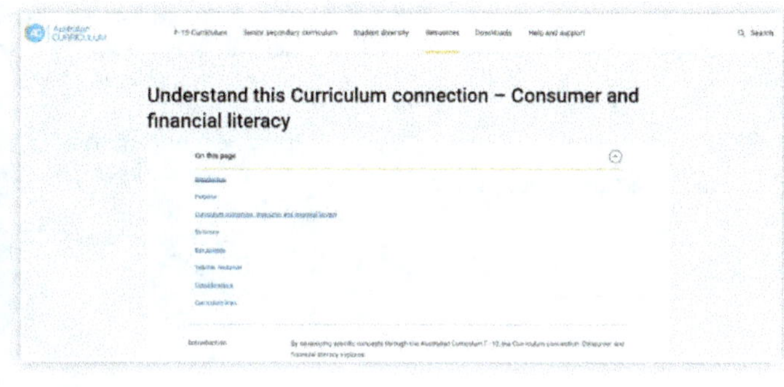

HASS
Economics and Business

STRAND / SUB-STRAND	CONTENT DESCRIPTIONS
Knowledge and understanding	The role of Australia's financial sector and its effect on economic decision-making by individuals, businesses, and global markets (AC9HE9K01).
	How economic decision-making involves the interdependence of consumers, businesses, the financial sector, and government (AC9HE9K02).
	The reasons Australia trades with other nations, and the patterns of trade between Australia and Asia (AC9HE9K03).
	Processes that businesses use to create and maintain competitive advantage, including the role of entrepreneurs (AC9HE9K04).
	How individuals and businesses manage consumer and financial risks and rewards (AC9HE9K05).
	The ways that government intervenes in the economy to improve economic performance and living standards within Australian society (AC9HE10K02).
	Factors that influence major consumer and financial decisions, and the short- and long-term consequences of these decisions (AC9HE10K03).
	The importance of Australia's superannuation system and how this system affects consumer and financial decision-making (AC9HE10K04).

HASS
Economics and Business

STRAND / SUB-STRAND	CONTENT DESCRIPTIONS
Skills Evaluating, concluding, and decision-making	Develop and evaluate a response to an economic and business issue, using cost-benefit analysis or criteria to decide on a course of action (AC9HE9S04).
	Develop and evaluate a response to an economic and business issue, using cost-benefit analysis or criteria to decide on a course of action (AC9HE10S04).
Skills Communicating	Create descriptions, explanations, and arguments, using economic and business knowledge, concepts, and terms that incorporate and acknowledge research findings (AC9HE9S05).
	Create descriptions, explanations, and arguments, using economic and business knowledge, concepts, and terms that incorporate and acknowledge research findings (AC9HE10S05).
Skills Questioning and researching	Develop and modify questions to investigate a contemporary economic and business issue (AC9HE9S01).
	Locate, select, and analyse information and data from a range of sources (AC9HE9S02).
	Develop and modify questions to investigate a contemporary economic and business issue (AC9HE10S01).
	Locate, select, and analyse information and data from a range of sources (AC9HE10S02).
Skills Interpreting and analysing	Interpret information and data, explaining economic and business issues, trends, and economic cause-and-effect relationships, and make predictions about consumer and financial impacts (AC9HE9S03).
	Interpret information and data, explaining economic and business issues, trends, and economic cause-and-effect relationships, and make predictions about consumer and financial impacts (AC9HE10S03).

HASS
Geography

STRAND / SUB-STRAND	CONTENT DESCRIPTIONS
Knowledge and understanding of Geographies of interconnections	The effects on places of people's travel, recreational, cultural, or leisure choices, and the strategies for managing the impacts on these places (AC9HG9K06).
	The ways that places and people are interconnected with other places through trade in goods and services, at all scales (AC9HG9K07).
	The impacts of the production and consumption of goods on places throughout the world, and strategies to manage sustainability in these places (AC9HG9K08).
Skills Concluding and decision-making	Evaluate data and information to justify conclusions (AC9HG9S04).
	Develop and evaluate strategies using environmental, economic, or social criteria; recommend a strategy and explain the predicted impacts (AC9HG9S05).
	Evaluate data and information to justify conclusions (AC9HG10S04).

DIGITAL TECHNOLOGIES

STRAND / SUB-STRAND	CONTENT DESCRIPTIONS
Knowledge and understanding Digital systems	Investigate how hardware and software manage, control, and secure access to data in networked digital systems (AC9TDI10K01).
	Investigate how hardware and software manage, control, and secure access to data in networked digital systems (AC9TDI10K01).
Process and production skills Privacy and security	Develop cyber security threat models, and explore a software, user, or software supply chain vulnerability (AC9TDI10P13).
	Apply the Australian Privacy Principles to critique and manage the digital footprint that existing systems and student solutions collect (AC9TDI10P14).
Process and production skills Evaluating	Evaluate existing and student solutions against the design criteria, user stories, possible future impact, and opportunities for enterprise (AC9TDI10P10).
Process and production skills Collaborating and managing	Select and use emerging digital tools and advanced features to create and communicate interactive content for a diverse audience (AC9TDI10P11).
	Use simple project management tools to plan and manage individual and collaborative agile projects, accounting for risks and responsibilities (AC9TDI10P12).

DESIGN AND TECHNOLOGIES

STRAND / SUB-STRAND	CONTENT DESCRIPTIONS
Knowledge and understanding Technologies and society	Analyse the impact of innovation, enterprise, and emerging technologies on designed solutions for global preferred futures (AC9TDE10K01).
Process and production skills Collaborating and managing	Develop project plans for intended purposes and audiences to individually and collaboratively manage projects, taking into consideration time, cost, risk, processes, and production of designed solutions (AC9TDE10P05).
	Select and use emerging digital tools and advanced features to create and communicate interactive content for a diverse audience (AC9TDI10P11).

STRAND / SUB-STRAND	CONTENT DESCRIPTIONS
Number	Recognise that the real number system includes the rational numbers and the irrational numbers, and solve problems involving real numbers using digital tools (AC9M9N01).
Algebra	Use mathematical modelling to solve applied problems involving growth and decay, including financial contexts; formulate problems, choosing to apply linear, quadratic, or exponential models; interpret solutions in terms of the situation; evaluate and modify models as necessary and report assumptions, methods and findings (AC9M10A04).
	Use mathematical modelling to solve applied problems involving change, including financial contexts; formulate problems, choosing to use either linear or quadratic functions; interpret solutions in terms of the situation; evaluate the model and report methods and findings (AC9M9A05).
Measurement	Use mathematical modelling to solve practical problems involving direct proportion, rates, ratios, and scale, including financial contexts; formulate the problems and interpret solutions in terms of the situation; evaluate the model and report methods and findings (AC9M9M05).
	Interpret and use logarithmic scales in applied contexts involving small and large quantities and change (AC9M10M02).
Statistics	Analyse reports of surveys in digital media and elsewhere for information on how data was obtained to estimate population means and medians (AC9M9ST01).
	Plan and conduct statistical investigations involving the collection and analysis of different kinds of data; report findings and discuss the strength of evidence to support any conclusions (AC9M9ST05).
	Use mathematical modelling to solve applied problems involving growth and decay, including financial contexts; formulate problems, choosing to apply linear, quadratic, or exponential models; interpret solutions in terms of the situation; evaluate and modify models as necessary and report assumptions, methods, and findings (AC9M10A04).

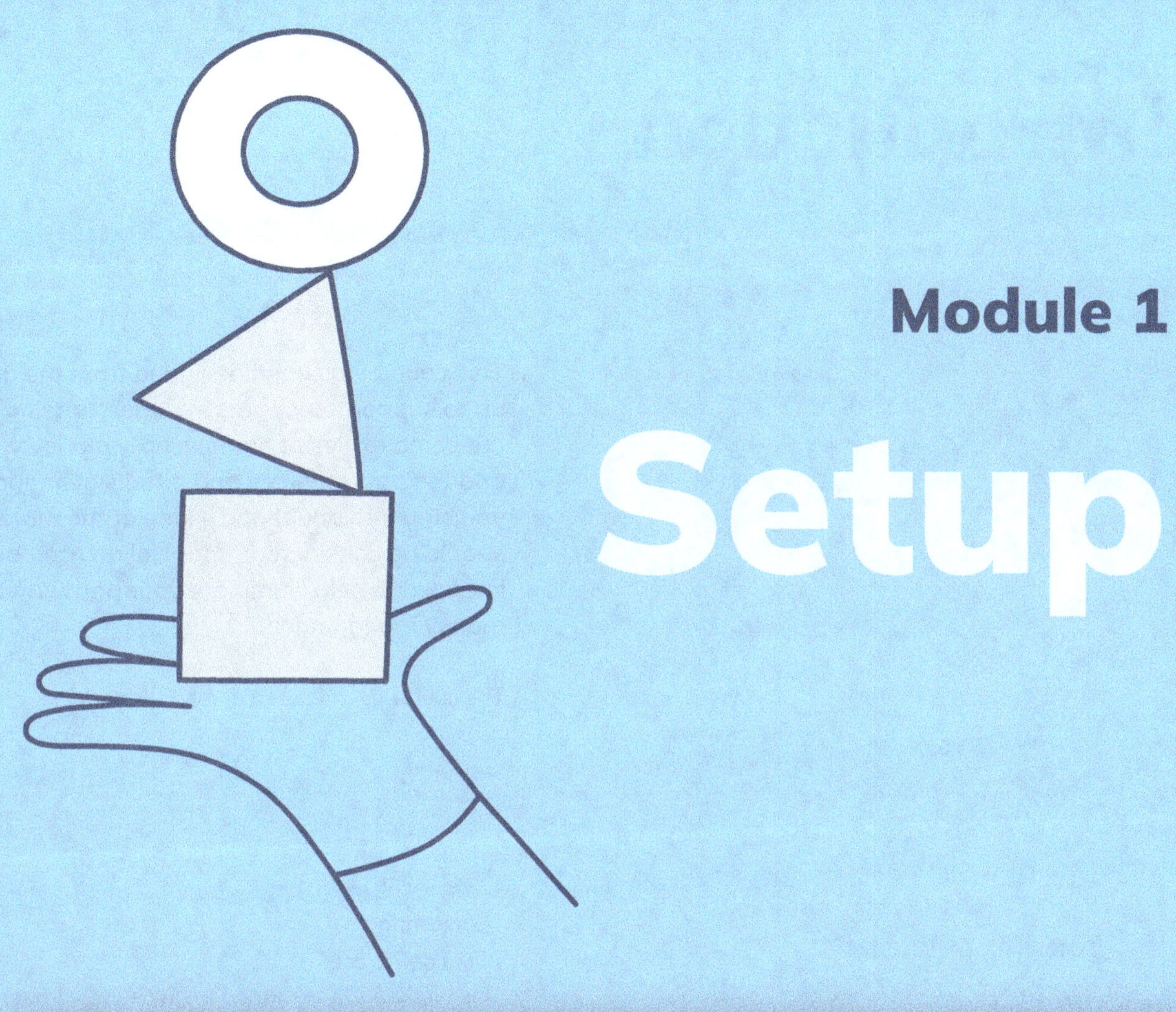

Module 1

Setup

Topic 1
Introduction

Welcome to Financial Success.

This course has been designed from the ground up to support teenagers in understanding some of the complexities of finance, how money works and the opportunities and pitfalls of finance as you step into adulthood. None of the material should be considered "financial advice", but it's intended to help illuminate your pathway to sound money management.

The course is structured across six modules:

- Setup
- Earning
- Saving
- Spending
- Investing
- Major Project

This workbook is designed to guide you through each of the concepts and directs you to a range of online sources to explore further. At the conclusion of the course, you have the option of completing an online examination that covers material across the entire course.

Micro-credentials are recognised opportunities to complete formal study in smaller chunks. In this way, you can build your professional portfolio of learning and gain credentials over time.

The next few pages are a pre-test and should be completed to the best of your ability without help from others or the internet. By the end of the course, you should be able to answer all of the questions confidently.

Learning Objective

By the end of this lesson students will be able to:

- Outline the structure and goals of the course
- Identify personal goals for the course
- Establish a USI

Key Terms

- USI
- Micro credential
- Financial Success

QUESTION	ANSWER
1. What is the difference between a debit card and a credit card?	
2. What is the difference between Income Tax and GST?	
3. Describe the concept of compound interest.	
4. What are shares?	
5. Write a summary of what you know about superannuation.	
6. What is a Tax File Number, and who needs one?	
7. What is the difference between a casual job and a part-time job?	
8. Is renting an item or buying an item better?	
9. How might interest rates be different between a personal loan and a mortgage?	

Topic 1 Introduction

QUESTION	ANSWER
10. What is a budget?	
11. Who spends tax income, and what do they spend it on?	
12. What is cryptocurrency?	
13. What information would you expect to see on a payslip?	
14. How is a transaction account different from a savings account?	
15. What is a credit score?	

Personal Reflection: What does financial success look like for me?

Australian Qualifications Framework

USI Unique Student Identifier

The Australian Government established a Unique Student Identifier in 2015. This system allows every Australian to have a number that they provide to learning institutions. The purpose is to keep all your qualifications recorded in one place. Over your educational journey, you may attain credentials within the Australian Qualifications Framework (AQF), ranging from Year 12 equivalency through to Doctorate-level studies.

Micro-credentials are designed to support learning toward these qualifications and are often recognised as addressing elements of a course within a given pattern of study.

To create a USI or find your USI, go to the following website: https://www.usi.gov.au/

Record your USI inside the front cover of this book.

Summary Points

- Your definition of financial success will be different from the next person's. It comes down to your priorities in life.
- Understanding a range of key terms and concepts will help you achieve your financial success.

Topic 2

Bank Accounts
Types

Learning Objective

By the end of this lesson, students will be able to:

- Identify types of bank accounts and their differences.
- Define some of the key jargon in banking.

Key Terms

- Credit
- Debit
- Prepaid
- Fees
- Interest

Launch Activity
Brain Dump

In the space provided, write down all the words you can think of in 5 minutes that relate to bank accounts. You might think about types of accounts, who provides them, how you use them or tools to manage money (minimum 10 words).

The terms "Credit Card" and "Debit Card" are sometimes used interchangeably, but they are not the same. The cards themselves are just a way to interact with the account that lives with the bank or financial institution. In both the cases, there is usually a physical card with a series of numbers, an expiry date, and on the reverse a CVC (Card Verification Code). All three sets of numbers are needed to complete online transactions. The biggest difference between Credit and Debit is whose money you are using. With Debit accounts, you are using money you already have in that account. Credit cards work as a short-term loan using your provider's money up to a previously agreed amount, which you pay back at the end of the month, in full or in part, paying interest on the outstanding balance.

Credit Card

- Short Term Loan
- Needs to be paid off each month
- Pay interest on the unpaid balance
- Often connected to the brand Visa or Mastercard, but can include others, such as Diners Club or American Express
- Can be used in store, online, or via phone app
- May require PIN, Biometrics, or a signature, depending on transaction amount.
- Can often include a transaction fee when used in-store, such as 1%.

Debit Card

- Can only use money you have in the account
- May charge overdraft, if you try to use more than you have
- Usually connected to the brand Visa or Mastercard
- Can be used in store, online or via phone app
- Requires the use of a PIN or biometrics
- May not include a transaction fee so long as you select debit. A number of cards will let you treat the debit card as either credit or debit. As a rule of thumb, if you are tapping it will process as a credit transaction even if it is using money from your own account.

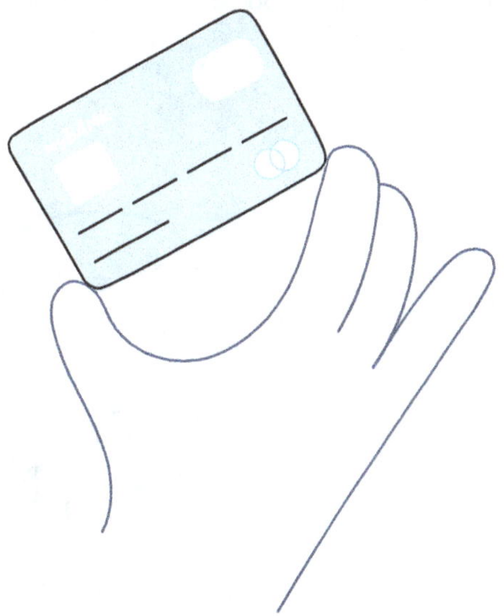

Topic 2 Bank Accounts
Types

Coffee Case Study

Your local Coffee Shop sells a large flat white for $5. You don't have cash and so you have three payment options.

1. Insert your debit card and enter your P.I.N.
2. Tap your phone and pay a $1 surcharge.
3. Tap your card and pay a 1% surcharge.

Use the following webpage to support your answers:

https://www.accc.gov.au/consumers/pricing/card-surcharges

QUESTIONS:

1. Which option would be considered illegal by the Australian Competition and Consumer Commission? Why?
2. Which option is the most expensive?
3. Which option do you normally take when in store?

Gift Cards

Gift cards are like debit cards insofar as there is an amount already put aside that can be spent. That amount can only be spent in the shop with the business nominated, and they will often have an expiry date after which any remaining balance is forfeited. They can also be difficult to spend the exact amount on the card.

Pre-Paid Cards

Many families have purchased prepaid cards for children to use. These are marketed as a way to teach children about the importance of saving and a way to transfer pocket money for use at school canteens or in shops. They are effectively prepaid debit cards designed for children. There are fees and charges associated with running these cards.

QUESTION	GIFT CARDS	PREPAID CARDS
Identify an example of these cards.		
List 2 advantages or situations in which they are useful.		
List 2 drawbacks of each card.		

TERM	MEANING
BSB	A 6-digit number that represents the Bank, State, and Branch from which a bank account is opened.
Account Number	A 9-digit number that identifies your specific account.
Card Number	This number is different from the above and is typically on the front/back of a debit or credit card.
CVC	A 3-digit number on the back of the card; used online as verification.
Expiry	Usually in MM/YY form. Cards typically expire every few years.

Summary Points

- Debit accounts use your existing money.
- Credit accounts are like a short-term loan using the institution's money.
- Some debit cards can operate as either credit or debit.
- Your payment method will incur different costs depending on your selected payment method.
- Gift cards and prepaid cards use pre-committed money, but each has advantages and disadvantages.

Topic 3

Bank Accounts
Comparing and Selecting

Learning Objective

By the end of this lesson students will be able to:

· Compare bank account products and recognise differences and similarities.

· Use comparison websites (e.g. Canstar, Finder, RateCity) to research and evaluate bank account options.

· Apply this information to their personal context.

Key Terms

· Transaction account
· Transaction fees
· Monthly Fees
· PAYID
· Google/Apple Wallet
· ATM
· Savings Accounts

Launch Activity
Reflection

Thinking about your own financial needs and habits, what would be most important to you when choosing a bank/financial institution and opening an account?

List the features you would want (e.g. debit card access, no fees, mobile app, high interest on savings accounts) and explain why each one matters to you.

FEATURE ONE

FEATURE TWO

FEATURE THREE

FEATURE FOUR

FEATURE FIVE

Banks and financial institutions offer a range of accounts and services to help people manage their money, and understanding the differences between them is key to making financial choices. Savings accounts are designed to help you grow your money over time. They often offer interest, sometimes bonus interest if you save regularly and avoid withdrawals, and are usually fee-free for young people. Many savings accounts also include goal-setting tools that let you track progress toward things like a new phone, holiday, or emergency fund.

Transaction accounts, on the other hand, are used for everyday spending and receiving money. These accounts typically come with a debit card that allows you to tap, swipe, or shop online using your own money. Most youth-friendly transaction accounts have no monthly fees and offer free access to your bank's ATMs.

Online and mobile banking features make it easy to check your balance, transfer money, and manage your spending on the go.

As you get older, you may also explore credit and loans, which involve borrowing money that must be paid back later, usually with interest. This includes credit cards, personal loans, and buy now, pay later services like Afterpay. While these options can be helpful, they also come with responsibilities. It's important to understand repayment rules, interest rates, and fees to avoid debt stress. Managing credit wisely and paying bills on time helps build a good credit history, which can be important for future financial goals like renting, buying a car, or applying for a mortgage.

Complete the table below with key points about the function and features of Transactions, Savings, and Credit/Loan Accounts:

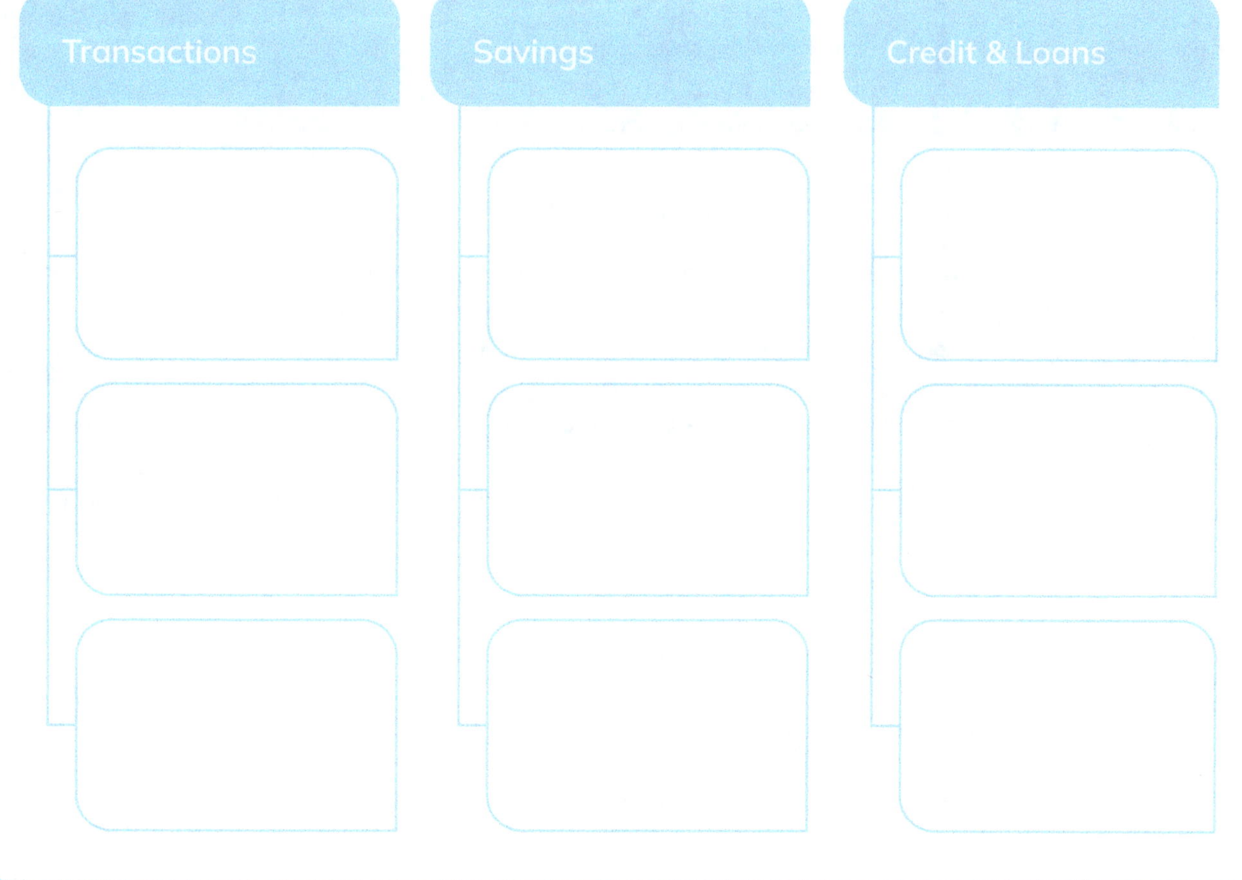

Topic 3 Bank Accounts
Comparing and Selecting

When choosing a bank account, it's important to understand key features and fees that affect how you manage your money. These include monthly fees, ATM charges, international transaction costs, and EFTPOS merchant fees. Useful tools like savings goal trackers, linked accounts, online/app access, and PAYID can help you stay in control and build smart habits. In this activity, you'll match each explanation or definition listed to its correct banking term or idea in the table above. This will help you recognise what to look for when comparing financial products and services.

TERMS

Monthly Fee	International ATM Fee	Savings Goal Tools
International Transaction Fee	Linked Transaction Account	PAYID
Own Network ATM Fee	EFTPOS Usage Fee (Merchant Fee)	Online/App Access

TERMS	EXPLANATION/DEFINITIONS
	A fast and secure way to receive money using your phone number or email instead of a BSB.
	A store may pass on a small cost when you tap or insert your card to pay.
	Banking app features that help you set and track savings goals like a digital piggy bank.
	A savings account connected to your spending account for easy transfers and automation.
	A fee charged when you buy something online or overseas using your card.
	A fee for using an ATM that belongs to your bank, usually free, but worth checking.
	A regular charge taken from your account each month, just for having the account open.
	Allows you to manage your money anytime via your bank's website or mobile app.
	A fee charged when withdrawing cash from an ATM in another country

Research Task: Comparing Bank Accounts

In this activity, you'll explore different banks and the products they offer, specifically savings accounts and transaction accounts. Your goal is to compare these accounts and decide which ones best suit your personal needs.

INSTRUCTIONS:

> **Choose 2–3 banks or financial institutions to research.**
  You can use comparison websites like Canstar or Finder to help you.

> For each bank, find one **savings account** and one **transaction account** that are suitable for young people or students.

> Look closely at the features of each account. These might include:
  · Monthly fees
  · ATM access
  · Interest rates
  · Online/app access
  · Savings goal tools

> Fill in the table with your findings. Rank these against the personal banking needs you outlined on the first page of the module.

BANK & ACCOUNT

FEATURES

RANK

BANK & ACCOUNT

FEATURES

RANK

BANK & ACCOUNT

FEATURES

RANK

BANK & ACCOUNT

FEATURES

RANK

Summary Points

· Different products will target different needs (know your needs first!)

· Beware of fees

· Continue to review what products you are using to ensure they meet your needs and match your lifestyle

Topic 4

Government Engagement

Learning Objective

By the end of this lesson students will be able to:

- Describe how a Tax File Number and Medicare Number are used.
- Describe the function of the My Gov Portal (Australia) and the relevant State Government Portal e.g. NSW, Victoria, etc.

Key Terms

- Tax File Number (TFN)
- Australian Taxation Office (ATO)
- Medicare

Activity

There is an old saying
"Only two things are certain in life... death and taxes".

While no one likes paying tax, it is important. For each of the following stand-points dot point some arguments for and against in the boxes.

Everyone should pay **equal** tax

Everyone should pay **what they want** in tax

Everyone should pay tax **according to their wealth**

Tax File Number

- A Tax File Number (TFN) is your personal reference number in the tax and superannuation systems.

- It is free to apply for a TFN.

YOUR TFN IS:

- A unique number (usually nine digits).
- An important part of your identity.
- Yours for life – You keep your TFN even if you change jobs or name, move interstate, or go overseas.

You, your employers, and the Government use that number to keep track of how much money you earn and how much tax you should pay. It is also used to identify you when it comes to government benefits, such as Youth Allowance.

HOW TO APPLY FOR A TFN?

You can apply for a TFN digitally if you are 15 Years old and hold an Australian Passport using the Digital ID App. Alternatively, you can apply using the forms on the ATO website:

https://www.ato.gov.au/individuals-and-families/tax-file-number/apply-for-a-tfn

The following video talks you through the steps to apply for a TFN using the paper forms:

https://youtu.be/ajUrEqimozk?si=-HsSq4n1IAdF0ulV

Bulk billing means you don't have to pay for your medical service from a health professional. They bill the Government instead, and they accept the Medicare benefit as full payment for the service.

Not all health professionals bulk bill. You should check if yours does when you make an appointment. A 'gap' payment is the difference between what Medicare will pay the doctor and what they are charging. You pay the gap.

Medicare

Medicare is Australia's universal health insurance scheme. It guarantees all Australians (and some overseas visitors) access to a wide range of health and hospital services at low or no cost.

Medicare pays for some or all of the costs of various medical services, including services delivered in public and private hospitals. It ensures all Australians have equitable access to health care when they need it, regardless of where they live or their ability to pay.

You must present your Medicare card when you:

- see a doctor
- go to a hospital as a public patient
- get a medical test done
- get prescription medicines listed on the PBS.

Not all health practitioners bulk bill, so always check what you will have to pay when making your appointment.

Research Task:
Does your GP bulk bill?

WHY WOULD YOU GO TO A DOCTOR WHO BULK BILLS?

WHY WOULD YOU GO TO A DOCTOR WHO DOES NOT BULK BILL AND YOU NEED TO PAY THE GAP?

Topic 4 Government Engagement

Digital access to Government services is becoming more important. There are 3 levels of Government in Australia each with their own portals and apps. Research for where you live what portals exist and what they are used for. Portals can include websites or phone apps.

GOVERNMENT LEVEL	PORTALS	USES
Federal	myGov App My ID App Medicare App	
State	Service NSW	
Local	(Check your council website)	

Summary Points

- Your definition of financial success will be different from the next person's. It comes down to your priorities in life.
- Understanding a range of key terms and concepts will help you achieve your financial success.

Review

Glossary Terms

TERM	DEFINITION
BSB	A 6-digit number that represents the Bank, State, and Branch from which a bank account is opened.
Account Number	A 9-digit number that identifies your specific account
Card Number	This number is different from the BSB and Account Number and is typically on the front / back of a debit or credit card.
CVC	A 3-digit number on the back of the card used online as verification
Expiry	Usually in MM/YY form. Cards typically expire every few years.
ATM	Automated Teller Machine
TFN	Tax File Number
ATO	Australian Taxation Office
Debit Card	A payment card linked directly to your Transaction Account; allows you to spend only the money you own.
Credit Card	A card that facilitates a short-term loan from the bank; the money must be paid back, usually with high interest.
Transaction Account	An everyday bank account that is used for frequent activities like depositing wages, paying bills, and using a debit card.
USI	Unique Student Identifier; a reference number required by the Australian government to receive a formal qualification.
EFTPOS	Electronic Funds Transfer at Point of Sale; the system used in stores to process card payments directly from an account.

Chapter Summary

This module was your launchpad, setting the essential groundwork for financial success.

- Your Goals: You learned the importance of setting clear, measurable personal financial goals and how these objectives will guide your decisions throughout the course and your life.
- Banking Basics: We clearly defined the function of bank accounts and introduced critical banking jargon. Crucially, you learned to distinguish a debit card (spending your money) from a credit card (spending the bank's money, a loan that must be paid back with interest).
- Account Comparison: You gained skills in comparing bank accounts based on fees, interest offered, and features, ensuring you choose the best fit for your needs.
- Government Ready: You established a basic understanding of how individuals interact financially with the government, including the necessary step of setting up your Unique Student Identifier (USI).
- Action Item: Make sure you've researched and noted down the pros and cons of two different bank accounts and confirmed your USI status.

Further Links

https://www.accc.gov.au/consumers/pricing/card-surcharges

https://moneysmart.gov.au/banking

https://moneysmart.gov.au/credit-cards

https://www.ato.gov.au/single-page-applications/iar

Earning

Learning Outcomes:

LO1
Demonstrate personal financial management skills by applying knowledge of budgeting, saving, earning, and spending to real-world scenarios.

LO5
Reflect on the ethical and social implications of financial decisions, considering the impact on self, community, and the environment.

Overview:

This module introduces the approaches to earning money through employment.

5	Job Types
6	Introduction to Tax
7	Payslips and Tax Returns
8	Earning Money Online

Job Types

Activity

If you could earn money doing anything for the next 6 months, what would it be, and how would it fit into your life?

WRITE DOWN:

· What key activities the job would involve?

· Working in a team or individually?

· If the job would be casual, part time, full time, gig-based or your own business and Why?

Discuss with a partner your answer and why you picked the job type (e.g. flexibility, money, passion etc.)

Learning Objective

By the end of this lesson students will be able to:

· Understand the differences in job types
· Identify the strengths and weakness between casual, part time, full time, gig and running your own business as earning opportunities

Key Terms

· Casual
· Part time
· Full time
· Gig

Understanding job types helps you choose work that fits into your lifestyle, values, and goals. These may change over time, and you may also complete a mixture of these throughout your life. Below are overviews of the main types of jobs where you can earn an income.

Casual Work

- Think: flexible hours, short shifts, and no set schedule.
- You might work weekends, holidays, or just when the boss needs you.
- You get paid a higher hourly rate (called a casual loading) because you don't get paid sick leave or holiday leave.
- Example: Working at a café on Saturdays or helping out at a retail store during school holidays.

Full-Time Work

- Think: 9 to 5, Monday to Friday (or similar).
- You work around 38 -40 hours a week.
- You get full benefits like paid leave and job security.
- Example: A full-time apprentice, office assistant, or tradie working every weekday.

Part-Time Work

- Think: regular hours, but fewer than full-time.
- You have a set schedule (like 3 days a week or afternoons only).
- You get benefits like paid sick leave and holiday leave, just like full-time workers – but in smaller amounts.
- Example: Working at a supermarket after school or tutoring younger students a few times a week.

Gig Work

- Think: short jobs, apps, and side hustles.
- You work when you want, often through platforms like Uber, Airtasker, or Fiverr.
- You're usually paid per task, not hourly, and you don't get employee benefits.
- Example: Delivering food, editing videos, or designing logos for people online.

Running Your Own Business

- Think: boss mode activated.
- You create your own product or service and earn money from customers.
- You manage your own schedule, income, and responsibilities (including tax and super).
- Example: Selling handmade jewellery online, mowing lawns, or starting a tutoring service.
- You will need an ABN (Australian Business Number)

Topic 5 Job Types

Case Study/Example

Tyler is 17 and in Year 11. He's juggling school, saving for a car, and figuring out what kind of work fits his life best.

JOB 1:
CASUAL RETAIL ASSISTANT

Tyler started working casually at a local clothing store on weekends. He liked the flexibility and the higher hourly pay, but sometimes his shifts were cancelled last-minute, and he couldn't rely on the income.

JOB 2:
PART-TIME TUTORING

To earn more consistently, Tyler took on a part-time tutoring job helping Year 7 students with maths. He works two afternoons a week and gets paid sick leave and holiday leave based on his hours.

SIDE HUSTLE:
SELLING ART PRINTS ONLINE

Tyler also runs a small online store selling digital art prints. He sets his own prices, promotes his work on social media, and manages orders himself. It's not steady income, but it's creative and rewarding.

WHAT ARE THE BENEFITS OF HAVING MORE THAN ONE JOB LIKE TYLER?

WHICH JOB TYPE DO YOU THINK WOULD SUIT YOU BEST RIGHT NOW—AND WHY?

WHAT CHALLENGES MIGHT TYLER FACE BALANCING SCHOOL AND WORK?

Thinking about the information presented to you and the case study, complete the table below with the pros and cons of each job type.

JOB TYPE	PROS	CONS
Casual		
Part Time		
Full Time		
Gig Work		
Own Business		

Additional Homework Task:

Write a to-do list of things you need to do to apply for a job, i.e., updated Resume/CV, have a TFN.

Summary Points

- Know the difference between **casual**, **part-time**, and **full-time** employment and how it affects your pay and entitlements.
- Each has unique strengths and challenges

Introduction to Tax

Learning Objective

By the end of this lesson students will be able to:

· Understand the role of ATO and Tax

· Differentiate between GST vs Income Tax

Key Terms

· GST

· Income Tax

· Capital Gains Tax (CGT)

· Fringe Benefits Tax (FBT)

Activity

Imagine you're the Treasurer and you have $100 billion to spend. How would you divide it between the following areas?

WRITE YOUR AMOUNTS AND EXPLAIN YOUR CHOICES

Healthcare

YOUR ALLOCATION ($B)

WHY (1 –2 SENTENCES)

Education

YOUR ALLOCATION ($B)

WHY (1 –2 SENTENCES)

Defence

YOUR ALLOCATION ($B)

WHY (1 –2 SENTENCES)

Transport (Roads, Railways, Buses)

YOUR ALLOCATION ($B)

WHY (1 –2 SENTENCES)

Welfare & Pensions

YOUR ALLOCATION ($B)

WHY (1 –2 SENTENCES)

Tax is money that people and businesses pay to the government. It's collected on things like wages, goods and services (GST), company profits, and even items brought into or out of the country (customs charges). This money helps fund important services we all use, like hospitals, schools, defence, national parks, and pensions.

Each year, the Australian Government creates a plan called the Budget, which explains:

- How will it collect tax money
- How much it expects to raise
- How it will spend that money across different areas (like health, education, and transport)
- The Budget is prepared by the Treasury Department and presented to Parliament by the Treasurer, who works with other ministers to decide how much funding each department will receive.

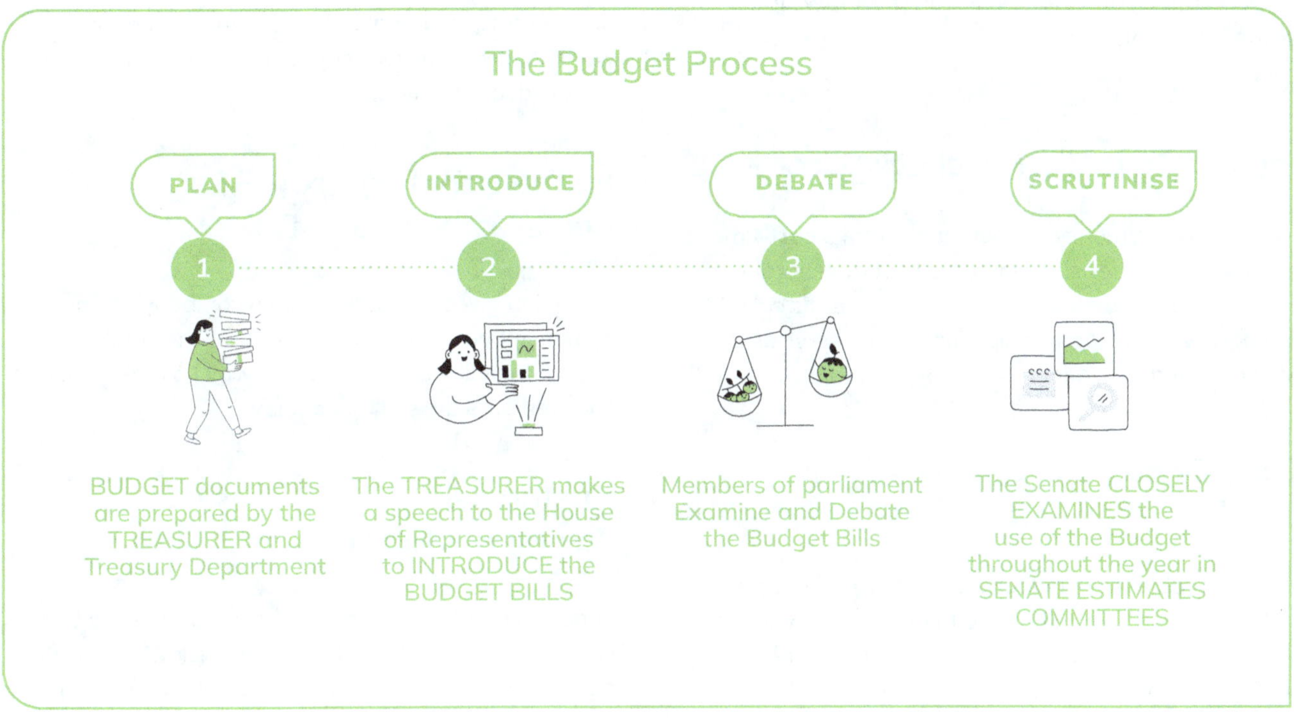

WRITE DOWN ALL THE DIFFERENT TYPES OF TAX THAT YOU HAVE HEARD OF (I.E., INCOME TAX, GST)

Topic 6 Introduction to Tax

There are many types of taxes in Australia, some may impact you currently, and some may impact you in the future. Knowing about taxes means you won't be caught off guard, and you'll know where your money is going. Below are some key examples.

Income Tax: The Paycheck Slice

When you earn money —whether it's from a part-time job, investments, or side gigs—the government takes a cut. The more you earn, the bigger the slice. It's called a progressive tax, and it helps fund public services like Medicare and education.

GST (Goods and Services Tax): The Everyday Tax

Bought bubble tea? Paid for a concert ticket? You've paid GST. It's a 10% tax added to most things you buy. Businesses earning over $75,000 a year must register for GST and pass it on to the government.

Corporate Tax: Big Business Pays Too

Companies in Australia pay tax on their pr ofits. The rate depends on how big they are and how much they earn. So yes, even your favourite sneaker brand or streaming service pays up.

Capital Gains Tax (CGT): Selling Stuff for Profit

Sold shares, property, or investments and made a profit? That 's a capital gain—and the government wants a piece. The longer you hold the asset, the better the tax deal usually is.

Fringe Benefits Tax (FBT): Perks Come with a Price

If your job gives you perks—like a company car, free gym membership, or concert tickets—the employer pay s Fringe Benefits T ax. It 's a way t o make sure non-cash rewards are still taxed fairly.

Customs & Excise Duties: Tax on the Extras

Imported goods like alcohol, tobacco, and fuel get hit with extra taxes. It's partly to raise money, and partly to discourage overuse (especially the unhealthy stuff).

Payroll Tax: Bosses Pay for Their Teams

Businesses pay payroll tax based on how much they spend on employee wages. It's different in each state, so a café in S y dney might pay a dif ferent rate than one in Perth.

Company & Resource Rent Taxes: Big Money from Big Resources

Companies that dig up Australia's natural resources (like miningor oil) pay extra taxes on the profits they make. It's called the resource rent tax, and it helps make sure the country benefits from its own land.

Quick Tax Quiz

1. **What type of tax do you pay when you earn money from a part-time job?**

   A.   Goods and Services Tax (GST)

   B.   Income Tax

   C.   Corporate Tax

   D.   Capital Gains Tax

2. **What is the standard rate of GST in Australia?**

   A.   15%

   B.   10%

   C.   5%

   D.   20%

3. **Which tax is applied when you sell something valuable like shares or property for a profit?**

   A.   Payroll Tax

   B.   Corporate Tax

   C.   Superannuation Tax

   D.   Capital Gains Tax

4. **Which of the following goes to local councils rather than State or Federal taxes?**

   A.   GST

   B.   FBT

   C.   Rates

   D.   Income Tax

Summary Points

- Tax helps fund the things we all use, like schools, hospitals, roads, and emergency services. It's how the government pays for public services.
- There are different types of taxes for different situations
- Understanding tax helps you make smarter money choices, whether you're earning, spending, saving, or starting a business. It's a key life skill for financial independence.

Topic 7

Payslips and Tax Returns

Learning Objective

By the end of this lesson students will
be able to:

· Understand how to read a payslip
  and what information is contained in
  payslips
· Understand the steps required to
  submit a tax return and high-level
  guidelines around the process to
  apply to individual circumstances

Key Terms

· YTD
· Gross Pay
· Net Pay
· Tax Deduction

TERM	DEFINITION
YTD	Year to Date (from the start of the financial year until today) Financial year starts 1 July and ends 30 June in Australia
Gross Pay	The total amount earnt before any deductions (like Tax or Super)
Net Pay	The total amount received to your bank account (take home pay after deductions)

Below is a sample first payslip for
Taylor Smith, who works after school
(part-time) in a café.

COMPLETE THE GREEN HIGHLIGHTED SECTIONS WITH THE
DOLLAR AMOUNTS THAT ARE MISSING:

Sunny Café

ABN: 12 345 678 910 123 High
Street, Sydney NSW 2000

Employee Name: Taylor Smith — Employee No.: 0157

Pay Period:
01 Sep 2025 – 14 Sep 2025

Pay Date:
15 Sep 2025

Employment Type: Part-time (After School)

Description	Rate	Hours	Amount
Ordinary Hours	$17.50	18	

Gross Pay = Amount	
Tax Withheld	$25.20
Net Pay = Gross Pay – Tax Withheld	
Superannuation (12%)	$37.80

YTD Gross	YTD Tax	YTD Super
	$25.20	$37.80

Topic 7 Payslips and Tax Returns

Every year, after the financial year has ended (1 July to 30 June), people in Australia complete a tax return to confirm to the government how much money they have earnt, and how much tax they have paid. While it is called a 'Tax Return', this does not necessarily mean everyone will receive a monetary return, it is 'returning information' to the government to confirm if you have paid the correct amount. If you have paid too much tax, you may receive a refund, but if you have paid too little, you may owe money.

A Tax return is just the name for the form you submit to report your income, and whether you receive or owe money depends on each individual situation. This process ensures money is collected to fund services as mentioned in the previous topic 'Introduction to Tax'.

There are a few ways to lodge a Tax return, including through a myGov account that is linked to the ATO or through a registered tax agent. If you are lodging a return yourself, you must lodge by 31 October, whereas an Agent can lodge after that date if engaged prior to 31 October.

Sometimes there may be costs associated with being able to earn money (e.g., as a hairdresser, scissors are a required tool that may not be supplied by an employer). The ATO approves a range of Tax Deductions, which is an expense that you are allowed to subtract from your income when working out how much tax you must pay.

FILL IN THE GAPS IN THE STATEMENTS BELOW:

If you earnt money during the last financial year (____ July to ____ June) you might need to lodge a tax return.

If you lodge a tax return yourself, it needs to be submitted by ________________.

A tax deduction is an expense you are allowed to ________________ from your ________________ when working out how much tax you must pay.

The following case studies will require you to look at the ATO website 'Deductions you can claim' to review what employees may be eligible to claim as a Tax Deduction.

Liam is 17 and works part-time as an apprentice chef in a busy Sydney restaurant. He wears a chequered uniform and steel-capped shoes every shift. He recently bought a new set of knives for work, costing $280, and subscribed to a monthly hospitality magazine to improve his skills. Liam also attends a short course on food safety that his employer recommended.

LIST THE TAX DEDUCTIONS LIAM MAY BE ELIGIBLE TO CLAIM.

Jayden is 17 and works casually at a sportswear store. He wears a branded uniform that's compulsory under the store's policy. He drives his own car to attend occasional stocktake shifts at other store locations. He keeps a logbook of these trips. Jayden also made a donation to a registered charity and pays union fees through his pay.

LIST THE DEDUCTIONS JAYDEN MAY BE ABLE TO CLAIM AND EXPLAIN WHY EACH ONE QUALIFIES.

Summary Points

- Payslips provide a breakdown of hourly pay rate, hours completed, payments made (including deductions – tax, superannuation, etc).
- Tax Returns are the form to complete and submit to the ATO to confirm that the tax paid is correct in line with earnings.

Earning Money Online

Learning Objective

By the end of this lesson, students will be able to:

- Identify opportunities and risks/realities of earning money online
- Describe considerations for earning online e.g., ABN, Digital footprint, Content Ownership, and link to Tax obligations

Key Terms

- ABN
- Digital Footprint
- Content ownership

Questions to discuss in pairs

· What are some ways people make money online?
· Do you follow any influencers, gamers, artists, or creators who earn money this way?
· What do you think is exciting about earning money online?
· What might be hard or risky?

COMPLETE THE TABLE BELOW:

OPPORTUNITIES	REALITIES/RISK

Topic 8 Earning Money Online

Activity
Earners

FOR EACH EARNER, ANSWER THE FOLLOWING
QUESTIONS: (NOTE HOW THIS PERSON EARNS MONEY)

1. What skills or tools do they need?

2. What challenges might they face?

3. What would you want to ask them?

PLAN	INTRODUCE	DEBATE	SCRUTINISE
1	2	3	4

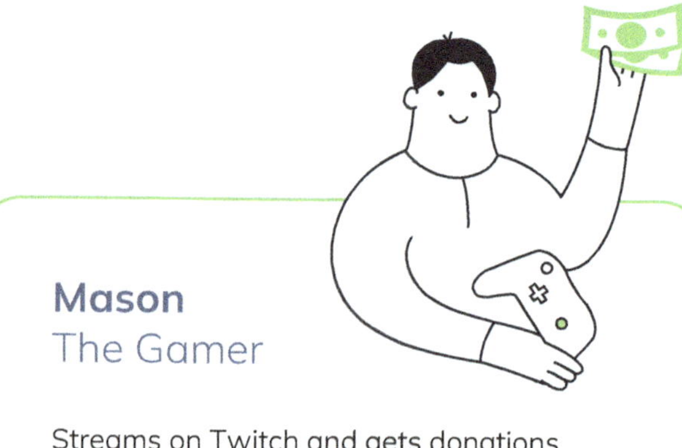

Mason
The Gamer

Streams on Twitch and gets donations.

1.

3.

Alisha
The Etsy Seller

Designs and sells digital art.

1.

2.

3.

Leo
YouTube Reviewer

Earns ad revenue and sponsorships

1. ________________________________

2. ________________________________

3. ________________________________

Julia
The TikTok Creator

Earns money through brand deals
and affiliate link

1. ________________________________

2. ________________________________

3. ________________________________

Important Terms to know...

ABN (AUSTRALIAN BUSINESS NUMBER)

- An ABN is an 11-digit number that identifies your business to the government and other businesses.
- If you start earning money online, you might need an ABN to register your work as a business.
- It doesn't replace your Tax File Number (TFN), but it helps with things like invoicing, claiming expenses, and avoiding confusion when working with clients.

DIGITAL FOOTPRINT

- Your digital footprint is the trail of information you leave online – like your social media posts, comments, search history, and even the websites you visit.
- When you earn money online, your digital footprint can affect your reputation, job offers, and how trustworthy you seem to customers or clients.

CONTENT OWNERSHIP

- Content ownership means having legal rights over the things you create – like videos, photos, designs, or written work.
- If you make something original (like a YouTube video or a digital artwork), you own it. But if you use someone else's content without permission, you could get into trouble.

Topic 8 Earning Money Online

Scam Spotting & Safe Choices

SCENARIO:

You receive a message on WhatsApp from someone claiming to be a recruiter. They offer $500/week to work from home with flexible hours and no experience needed. They ask you to send $50 to access training materials.

QUESTIONS:

- What are the red flags?
- What should you do next?
- How can you protect yourself from online scams?

Summary Points

- There are many ways to earn money online, but each comes with different skills, risks, and responsibilities.
- Protect your digital footprint, know your content rights, and consider getting an ABN if you're earning regularly.

CREATE A CHECKLIST OF THINGS TO LOOK FOR WHEN EVALUATING ONLINE WORK

Some example questions to answer could be:

Are there upfront fees?

Is the income too good to be true?

My Earning Online Safety Checklist

1.

2.

3.

4.

Review

Glossary Terms

TERM	DEFINITION
Casual Work	A job with flexible hours and no guaranteed shifts. You get paid a higher hourly rate but don't receive paid leave.
Part-time Work	A job with regular hours that are less than full-time. You get paid leave and other entitlements.
Full-time Work	A job with set hours (usually around 38 hours per week) and full employee benefits like paid leave and super
Gig Work	Short-term or task-based jobs, often through apps like Uber or Airtasker. You're usually self-employed and manage your own tax.
GST	Goods and Services Tax; A 10% tax added to most goods and services sold in Australia.
Income Tax	Tax paid on the money you earn from work, business, or investments. Taken out of your pay if you're an employee.
Capital Gains Tax (CGT)	Tax on the profit you make when selling assets like shares, property, or cryptocurrency.
Fringe Benefits Tax (FBT)	Tax paid by employers on extra benefits they give employees (e.g., company car, gym membership).
YTD	The total amount you've earned or paid in tax since 1 July of the current financial year.
Gross Pay	Your total earnings before tax and other deductions.
Net Pay	Your take-home pay after tax and deductions — what goes into your bank account.
Tax Deduction	An expense you can subtract from your income to reduce the amount of tax you pay (e.g., work tools, uniforms).
ABN	A number that identifies your business or freelance work. You need one to invoice or earn money as a sole trader.
Digital Footprint	The trail of data you leave online — including posts, likes, searches, and shared content.

Review

Chapter Summary

In this chapter, you have explored the world of work, tax, and digital income through four key topics. You commenced by examining different job types, including full-time, part-time, casual, contract, and self-employment, and how each affects pay, entitlements, and responsibilities. The chapter then introduced the basics of tax, explaining why we pay it, how income tax works, and when a tax return is required. Students learned how to read payslips and understand key terms like gross pay, net pay, and year-to-date (YTD) figures, as well as how to lodge a tax return using myTax. Finally, the chapter explored the opportunities and realities of earning money online, covering income from social media, content creation, and gig platforms, while highlighting the importance of declaring all income, understanding tax obligations, and maintaining digital safety.

Further Links

https://www.ato.gov.au/individuals-and-families/jobs-and-employment-types/new-to-tax-and-super

https://www.ato.gov.au/individuals-and-families/your-tax-return/how-to-lodge-your-tax-return/lodging-your-first-tax-return

Saving

Learning Outcomes:

LO1

Demonstrate personal financial management skills by applying knowledge of budgeting, saving, earning, and spending to real-world scenarios.

LO2

Analyse and evaluate financial products and services using critical thinking and cost-benefit analysis to make informed decisions.

Overview:

This module addresses matters around saving money and a person's capacity to use savings effectively.

Topic 9

Bank Accounts for Saving

Learning Objective

By the end of this lesson students will be able to:

- Identify key features to look for in Savings Accounts
- Explore and compare features in Saving Accounts

Key Terms

- Minimum spend/deposits
- Minimum balance

In Module One, we explored the difference **between** Transaction and Savings accounts. Put down key terms that you remember from each of the accounts in the mind-map below.

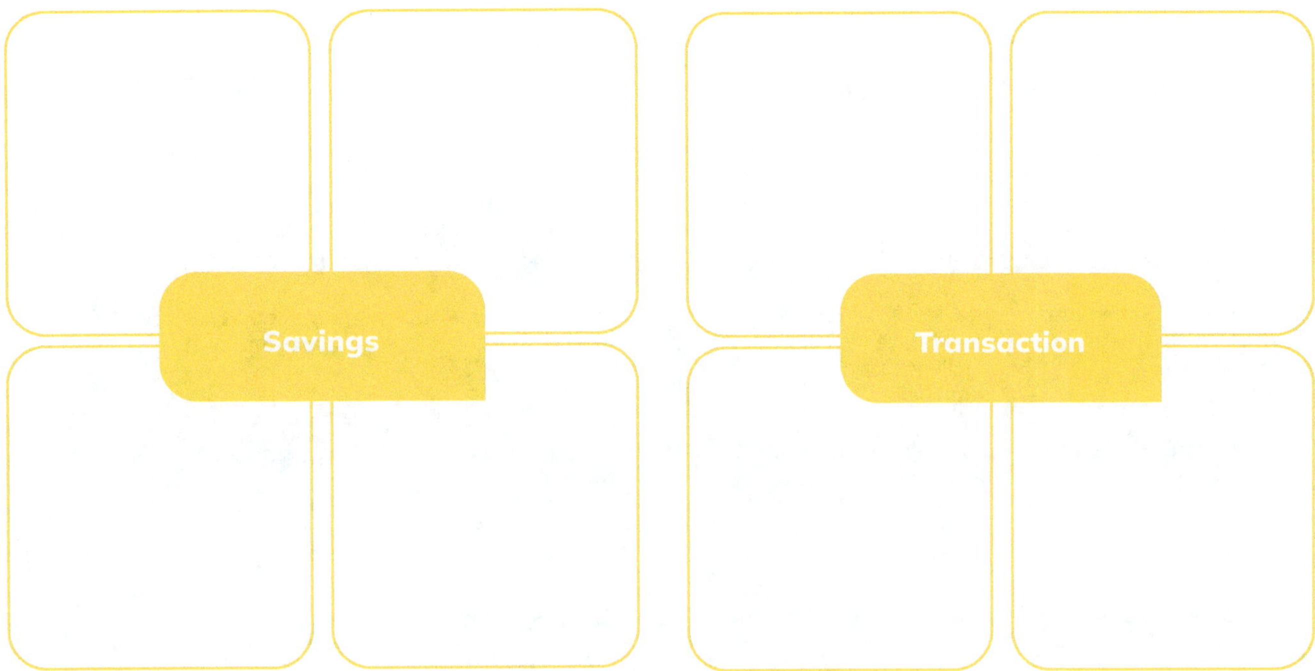

Savings Accounts can offer many features to help you achieve your goals. Some features are listed below:

HIGH INTEREST RATES

- The higher the interest rate, the more your savings grow over time
- Some accounts also offer bonus interest if you meet certain conditions (i.e., regular/minimum deposits and no withdrawals)

LOW OR NO FEES

- Some accounts may offer no monthly fees or transaction charges

EASY ACCESS/APP ACCESS/ONLINE BANKING

- You want to be able to easily check your balance and transfer money
- You may wish to manually transfer savings or set up an auto transfer (if you want an auto transfer, make sure the account has this feature)

RANK THE FEATURES OF A SAVINGS ACCOUNT FROM MOST TO LEAST IMPORTANT (TO YOU)

FEATURE	RANKING
High Interest Rate	
Bonus Interest	
Monthly Fees	
Withdrawal Limits	
Online Banking/App	
Savings Tools/Goal Tracker	
Minimum Deposit Requirements	

Topic 9 Bank Accounts for Saving

Savings Account Comparison

OPTION 1: GOAL GETTER SAVER	
Online banking/App:	Full-featured app with goal tracker, savings challenges, and reminders
Savings tools/goal tracker:	Built-in goal tracker with visual progress bars
Interest Rate:	2.5% p.a.
Bonus Interest:	Extra 1% if no withdrawals for 3 months
Monthly Fees:	$0 monthly fee
Withdrawal Limits:	Max 2 withdrawals/month to encourage saving
Minimum Deposit:	$10 to open account

OPTION 2: FREEDOM FLEX ACCOUNT	
Online banking/App:	Basic app with balance check and transfers
Savings tools/goal tracker:	Not included
Interest Rate:	1.8% p.a.
Bonus Interest:	None
Monthly Fees:	$0 monthly fee
Withdrawal Limits:	Unlimited withdrawals
Minimum Deposit:	No minimum deposit

OPTION 3: POWER INTEREST PLUS

Online banking/App:	Full-featured app with budgeting tips
Savings tools/goal tracker:	Basic goal tracker
Interest Rate:	3.5% p.a.
Bonus Interest:	Extra 2% if you deposit $20/month consistently
Monthly Fees:	$2 monthly fee
Withdrawal Limits:	Max 1 withdrawal/month
Minimum Deposit:	$50 to open an account

Further questions to consider

· How much will it cost me to have the account, per year and per month?
· Do accounts with higher account-keeping fees provide me a greater return (interest) on my savings?
· Are there other options to consider once I have hit my savings amount? (research Term Deposits)

Summary Points

· A savings account is designed to help you grow your money over time with interest, while a transaction account is for everyday spending.
· When comparing savings accounts, look at features like interest rates, bonus interest conditions, fees, withdrawal limits, and whether it includes tools like goal trackers or a banking app to help you stay on track.

Topic 10

Setting Savings Goals

Learning Objective

By the end of this lesson students will be able to:

· Understand the purpose and benefits of setting short-term and long-term savings goals

· Identify personal wants vs. needs to prioritise savings effectively

Key Terms

· SMART Goal
· Priority
· Short Term
· Long Term

Below is a list of items that you may look to purchase in the future. There is space for you to put in two extra items not listed. Fill in what you believe the cost would be, and your choice between:

D Dream goal (big future goal)

S Save for later

P Priority in the next few months

FEATURE	CHOICE	PRICE
New phone		
Car		
Emergency Fund		
Holiday		
Concert Ticket		
Apartment bond/rent		

Choose one item you marked as "Save for later" or "Dream goal."
· Why is it important to you?
· How long do you think it would take to save for it?
· What might help you stay motivated to reach that goal?

EITHER JOT DOWN YOUR THOUGHTS OR PAIR UP TO SHARE AND DISCUSS.

Module 3 Saving

Topic 10 Setting Savings Goals

Setting savings goals can seem daunting, but it is a great way to stay motivated, focused, and in control of your money. Below are some simple steps to help turn your goals into a clear, achievable plan.

Define your Goal

- Decide what you're saving for. Be specific whether it's a new phone, a car, a holiday, or an emergency fund.

Set a Target Amount

- Figure out how much you'll need. Break it into smaller chunks if it feels too big

Set a Timeline

- Choose when you want to reach your goal.
- Short-term: within 1 year
- Medium-term: 1–5 years
- Long-term: 5+ years

Calculate Monthly Savings

- Divide your target amount by the number of months until your deadline.

Automate Your Savings

- Set up automatic transfers so money goes straight into your savings—no thinking needed!

Track Your Progress

- Check in regularly. Celebrate milestones and adjust your plan if needed

SMART Savings Goal Template

COMPLETE THE TEMPLATE BELOW AND SET YOUR FIRST SAVING GOAL

SMART STEP	QUESTION	ANSWER
Specific	What exactly do you want to save for?	
Measurable	How much money do you need?	
Achievable	How will you earn and how much will you save each week?	
Relevant	Why is this important to you?	
Time-bound	When do you want to reach your goal?	

Summary Points

- SMART savings goals help individuals create specific, measurable, achievable, relevant, and time-bound plans for saving money.
- Setting savings goals involves identifying short-term and long-term priorities and distinguishing between personal wants and needs.

Topic 11

Credit Scores

Credit scores can feel confusing; how can someone give you a score based on your money habits? And how do they even know what you're spending or saving? Your credit score is just a way for banks and lenders to figure out how reliable you are when it comes to borrowing money and paying it back. Let's break it down together using the KWL chart below.

K

____

K = WHAT I KNOW

____

____

____

W

Learning Objective

By the end of this lesson students will be able to:

· Understand what a credit score is, why they matters, and how it affects borrowing and financial opportunities.

· Identify the key behaviours that influence credit scores, such as paying bills on time and managing debt.

W = WHAT I WANT TO KNOW

____

____

____

L

L = WHAT I LEARNED

(COME BACK TO THIS AT THE END OF THE LESSON)

____

Key Terms

· Credit Score

____

What is a Credit Score?

A credit score is a number that shows how reliable you are with money, especially when it comes to borrowing and paying it back.

Banks and lenders use your credit score to decide if they'll give you a loan, credit card, or phone plan.

- The higher your score, the more trustworthy you seem. Your score is based on things like:
- How much money you've borrowed
- Whether you pay bills and loans on time
- How often you apply for credit

You can check your credit score for free, and it's a good idea to do this regularly. If your score is low, it might be harder to get approved for things like car loans or rental agreements in the future.

Understanding Credit Score Ranges

Excellent (800-1000)	This score shows you're well above average and considered reliable by lenders.
Very Good (700-799)	Your'e above average and likely to be approved for most types of credit.
Good (625-699)	Your'e in the average range and generally seen as a responsible borrower.
Fair (550-624)	Your'e score is below average, which may limit your options or lead to higher interest rates.
Low (0-549)	This score is considered poor and may make it harder to get approved.

Summary Points

- Scores can go up or down based on financial habits like paying bills on time or missing payments.
- Credit scores affect your ability to get loans, phone plans, or even rent a place in the future.
- A credit score is a number that shows how reliable someone is with borrowing and repaying money.

Topic 11 Credit Scores

You may not yet have enough credit history to have a Credit Score, but once you start having bills directed to your name, it is a good time to start checking your score!

IN THE TABLE BELOW, WRITE 'INCREASE' OR 'LOWER' PER SCENARIO AS TO HOW YOU THINK IT WOULD IMPACT A CREDIT SCORE.

SCENARIO	INCREASE OR LOWER CREDIT SCORE?
Missing payments or paying late	
Keeping credit card balances low	
Owing too much money compared to your credit limit	
Applying for lots of loans or credit cards at once	
Using credit responsibly over a long period	
Only applying for credit when you really need it	
Defaulting on a loan or having a debt sent to collections	

Spectrum Debate

AFTER EACH PROMPT, STUDENTS POSITION THEMSELVES ALONG THE SPECTRUM (E.G. STRONGLY AGREE
– AGREE – NEUTRAL – DISAGREE – STRONGLY DISAGREE) AND EXPLAIN THEIR REASONING.

Credit scores are a fair way to judge someone's financial responsibility.

STRONGLY AGREE | AGREE | NEUTRAL | DISAGREE | STRONGLY DISAGREE

REASON:

Teenagers should learn about credit scores before they leave school.

STRONGLY AGREE | AGREE | NEUTRAL | DISAGREE | STRONGLY DISAGREE

REASON:

A single missed payment shouldn't affect your credit score.

STRONGLY AGREE | AGREE | NEUTRAL | DISAGREE | STRONGLY DISAGREE

REASON:

People with low credit scores should pay higher interest rates.

STRONGLY AGREE | AGREE | NEUTRAL | DISAGREE | STRONGLY DISAGREE

REASON:

Credit scores give banks too much power over people's lives.

STRONGLY AGREE | AGREE | NEUTRAL | DISAGREE | STRONGLY DISAGREE

REASON:

Our credit score should include things like rent and phone bills.

STRONGLY AGREE | AGREE | NEUTRAL | DISAGREE | STRONGLY DISAGREE

REASON:

It's easy to improve your credit score if you try.

STRONGLY AGREE | AGREE | NEUTRAL | DISAGREE | STRONGLY DISAGREE

REASON:

Credit scores are more important than savings when planning for the future.

STRONGLY AGREE | AGREE | NEUTRAL | DISAGREE | STRONGLY DISAGREE

REASON:

Topic 12

Compound Interest

Learning Objective

By the end of this lesson students will be able to:

- Understand how compound interest grows savings over time and why starting early matters
- Calculate compound interest using simple examples and digital tools
- Compare savings outcomes with and without compound interest to make informed financial decisions

Key Terms

- Compound Interest
- Simple Interest

Video

My Five Cents: What is compound interest?

REFLECTING ON THIS VIDEO WRITE DOWN SOME POINTS FOR THE FOLLOWING QUESTIONS.

- What was the key insight you took away from the video?

- Are you still unsure about a topic mentioned in the video or would you like further time exploring something mentioned in the video?

- In a sentence write what you understand compound interest to be.

Compounding Interest on $100 at 10%

INITIAL	YR 1	YR 2	YR 3	YR 4	YR 5	YR 6	YR 7
Value at the start of the year	$100	$110	$121	$133	$146	$161	$177
Interest Earned over time	$10	$21	$33	$46	$61	$77	$95
Interest earned this year	$10	$11	$12	$13	$15	$16	$18

Discuss

· What if you took the interest out each year instead of leaving it in?

· If you took the interest out each year would the interest, be compound or simple interest?

Compound Interest

You earn interest on your original amount AND on the interest you've already earned.

Your money grows faster because each year builds on the last.

Simple Interest

You earn interest only on the original amount you put in (called the principal).

The interest stays the same each year.

Topic 12 Compound Interest

Calculating interest can be very mathematical, but there are several free websites that have their own compound interest calculators. Either using a website calculator (from a reputable website) or your own mathematics skills complete the problems below.

FILL IN THE TABLE BELOW COMPOUNDING INTEREST ON $150 AT 5%

INITIAL	YR 1	YR 2	YR 3	YR 4	YR 5	YR 6	YR 7
Value at the start of the year	$150						
Interest Earned over time							
Interest earned this year							

Simple vs Compound comparison

You save $200 with 5% interest.

· How much will you have after 3 years with simple interest?

· How much will you have after 3 years with compound interest?

Revisit your SMART Goal from Topic 10 with focus on your answers to MAT – write them down again.

SMART STEP	QUESTION	ANSWER
Measurable	How much money do you need?	
Achievable	How will you earn and how much will you save each week?	
Time-bound	When do you want to reach your goal?	

Imagine you are putting this money (above) into a savings account with a 5% interest rate. Will you reach your goal faster than originally set?

Utilise a free online compound interest calculator or your own mathematical skills.

Summary Points

- Compound interest helps your savings grow by adding interest on both your original money and the interest you've already earned.
- The earlier you start saving, the more your money can grow over time – making a big difference in the long run.

Review

Glossary Terms

TERM	DEFINITION
Minimum spend/deposits	The smallest amount of money you need to spend or deposit to unlock a benefit, like earning interest or getting a reward.
Minimum balance	The lowest amount of money you must keep in your account to avoid fees or earn interest.
Credit Score	A number that shows how reliable you are with borrowing and repaying money.
Compound Interest	Interest that grows not just on your original money, but also on the interest you've already earned—making savings grow faster over time.
Simple Interest	Interest that grows only on your original amount (the principal), staying the same each year.
Principal	The original amount of money deposited, invested, or borrowed before any interest is added or subtracted.
Bonus Interest	Extra interest added to a savings account when you meet certain monthly conditions, such as making a minimum deposit and making no withdrawals.
Liquidity	How easily an asset or money can be converted into immediate cash; money in a bank account is highly liquid.

Chapter Summary

In this chapter, you have explored the importance of saving
and how to make smart decisions with your money through
four key topics. You began by learning about different types of
bank accounts, including transaction and savings accounts,
and how each serves a different purpose in managing
and growing your money. The chapter then introduced the
concept of setting savings goals, encouraging you to think
about why you want to save, what you're saving for, and how
to stay motivated over time.

You also examined credit scores, what they are, why they
matter, and how your financial habits can affect your ability
to borrow money in the future. Finally, the chapter introduced
compound interest from a savings perspective, showing how
money can grow over time and why starting early makes a
big difference. These foundations help you understand how
saving works before moving into more complex topics like
loans and borrowing.

Further Links

https://moneysmart.gov.au/banking

https://moneysmart.gov.au/managing-debt/credit-scores-
and-credit-reports

https://files.moneysmart.gov.au/media/mfmd32me/
understanding-compound-interest-lesson-plan.pdf

https://moneysmart.gov.au/budgeting/compound-
interest-calculator

Spending

Learning Outcomes:

LO3

Understand and exercise roles, rights, and responsibilities as consumers in both physical and digital environments.

LO4

Communicate financial ideas and decisions effectively using appropriate terminology, digital tools, and data representations.

Overview:

This module seeks to establish basic concepts and develop an understanding of how banks and government relate to individuals.

Topic 13

Borrowing Money

Learning Objective

By the end of this lesson students will be able to:

· Identify key features to look for in Savings Accounts

· Explore and compare features in Saving Accounts

Key Terms

· Minimum spend/deposits
· Minimum balance

SOURCE OF FINANCE	WHAT DO YOU KNOW ABOUT THIS OPTION?
Bank Personal Loan	
Credit Card	
Pay Day Lender	
Pawn Shops (Cash Converters)	
Buy now-pay later services	
Loan from friends	
Loan from family	

Topic 13 Borrowing Money

For the services on the previous page, complete research to find out typical interest rates and unique conditions that could create additional costs. Your aim is to be able to describe each product using mathematical skills.

SOURCE OF FINANCE	TYPICAL INTEREST RATE	SUMMARY OF CONDITIONS THAT APPLY (WHAT HAPPENS IF THE LOAN CONDITIONS ARE NOT MET)
Bank Personal Loan		
Credit Card		
Pay Day Lender		
Pawn Shops (Cash Converters)		
Buy Now-Pay Later services		
Loan from friends		
Loan from family		

Zara

- Apprentice Plumber.
- Uses a car for work.
- Lives in parents' large home in Western Sydney.

Leo

- Computing Engineer.
- Lives in a studio apartment in the Inner City.
- Tends to eat meals at work due to long hours.

Mia

- Primary School Teacher
- Works and lives in the same suburb
- Lives in a unit above a shopping complex.
- Enjoys beach getaways each school holiday.

Toby

- Training to become a nurse.
- Education expenses are tough when only earning a casual wage through bar work.
- Living in a shared unit near uni.

PERSON	ITEM	BEST FINANCE OPTION	WORST FINANCE OPTION
Zara 18	Zara has a collection of second-hand tools her grandfather gave her to start her apprenticeship, but they are old and not the brands that others have. She would like to replace them all.		
Leo 17	Leo buys lots of meals through Uber Eats and wants to make sure he is getting the best value in terms of cost as well as bonus points.		
Mia 18	Mia is a responsible person with money for 10 weeks during term time, and then has a big blowout during school holidays on shopping and dining out.		
Toby 17	Toby's income is very unpredictable; some weeks the tips are better than others. He wants to manage his money through the tough weeks.		

Topic 13 Borrowing Money

Why is it an advantage to lenders when people don't make payments on time?

What is the relationship between how easy it is to secure a loan and the cost of the loan, i.e., is it more expensive to take out an easy loan?

What advice would you give about borrowing money?

Summary Points

- Always compare interest rates! Rates on a personal loan or credit card are usually much higher than those on a mortgage.
- Understand how the interest rate affects the total cost of borrowing.
- Be aware of the cost of not meeting payment requirements.

Topic 14

Interest

Launch Activity
Brain Dump

In the space provided write down all you can about interest when it comes to money. What is interest? Is it good or bad? Should interest rates be high or low? Who pays interest? Who receives interest?

Learning Objective

By the end of this lesson students will be able to:

- Describe the impact of loans to the total cost of ownership.
- Evaluate the cost and benefit of purchases using loans.

Key Terms

- Credit Score
- Credit History
- Interest Rate
- Total cost of ownership

Module 4 Spending

Topic 14 Interest

Interest coming to you is good. It is where a bank pays you a percentage for keeping money in an account with them.

In essence, interest is money paid to allow one party to use someone else's money.

Interest being paid by you is lost money. It is where you are paying a bank or similar for borrowing money from them.

EXAMPLES	YOU PUT MONEY IN SAVINGS WITH THE BANK	YOU BORROW MONEY FROM THE BANK
Initial amount	$100	$100
Interest Rate (simply calculated annually)	2% pa	6% pa
Amount after 12 Months	$102	$106

Case Study:
Kate the Real Estate Trainee

Kate is 19 years old and wants a good-looking car as a trainee Real Estate agent because no one wants to buy a house from someone who turns up in a bomb.

She will do a lot of city driving and needs some boot space for materials. She is confident that her job is secure, and she earns a good income of $68,000. Ironically, she lives at home because buying her own home seems a long way away. Saving has not been a priority yet because she has needed to buy a lot of new work clothes, although she has $10,000, which was gifted to her by a late grandparent to start her off in adult life. The absolute most she could put toward car payments would be $350 per fortnight, but that would impact her lifestyle.

Ideal New Car

- Kate would really like a Tesla Model Y which sells for $58,900.
- She is happy to invest her grandparents' gift in this purchase because she feels it will hold its value and will remind her of them every day.
- Being fully electric and hi-tech just fits her environmental ideals and personal style.

Ok New Car

- Kate has also looked at an MG3, which sells for $21,790.
- It's still a new car, and being small, it would really help getting into tight parking spots at open for inspection events in the inner city.
- The back seats would need to be laid down almost always to fit her work equipment, which would be painful picking up friends on the weekend or on the way to sports practice mid-week.

Good Second-Hand Car

- A neighbour is selling their 13-year-old Jeep Grand Cherokee for $10,000.
- They have looked after it, but with over 140,000km of driving it is showing its age.
- It has lots of space in the back for storage and would easily fit most of the netball team in comfort.
- It will be challenging to park at some open homes, and is the exact opposite of Kate's green preference in cars.
- In terms of client judgement, this car would be seen positively by prospective clients, as many of them would own something similar.

Topic 14 Interest

QUESTION	ANSWER	
How many years is a typical car loan in Australia?	Tesla:	
	MG:	
	Jeep:	
Using a loan calculator like the one at the bottom of the page, how much would fortnightly repayments be?	Tesla:	
	MG:	
	Jeep:	
Using the same calculator, how much interest will Kate pay assuming she makes the same repayments for the life of the loan?	Tesla:	
	MG:	
	Jeep:	
After 7 years, what costs will Kate have paid for each car? Consider Initial, interest, and maintenance costs.	Tesla:	
	MG:	
	Jeep:	

Recommend to Kate which car she should purchase, considering her needs, wants, and total cost of ownership

https://www.themutual.com.au/reusable-content/calculators/car-loan-repayment/

Summary Points

- Compound interest is great when saving, but can be dangerous if not controlled in spending.
- It is important to separate needs and wants when considering taking out a loan for a car, holiday, and especially when using credit cards.
- Minimum repayments do little to reduce the balance of a loan.

Topic 15

Short Term Loans

Learning Objective

By the end of this lesson students will be able to:

· Identify a range of short-term loan lenders.
· Compare services and make informed choices about the use of short-term loans.

Key Terms

· Interest payments
· Late fees
· Establishment fee

WITHOUT RESEARCH, IDENTIFY THE FOLLOWING PRODUCTS AS LOANS OR NOT LOANS

PRODUCT	LOAN	NOT SURE	NOT A LOAN
Pay in 4			
PayPal			
Payday lender			
Pawn shops like Cash Converters			
Buy Now Pay Later			
Uber Eats			
Credit Card			
Pay with cash			
Afterpay			
Debit Card			
Flybuys			
Lay-buy service through a shop			

Topic 15 Short Term Loans

Key Concepts

INTEREST RATE

· The amount the lender will add to your balance over time. If payments are not completed on time, this rate might change dramatically.

FEES AND CHARGES

· The amount the lender will charge for setting up the service or loan. This might be a per-transaction fee, a monthly fee, or other.

PAYMENT TERMS

· The period over which the loan occurs and the conditions that apply. There is often a significant amount of writing that can hide important details.

Group Task

In pairs or trios, research the cost of short-term loans by completing the following table. Each person is to complete the whole table in their book.

SERVICE	STANDARD INTEREST RATE	LATE PAYMENT INTEREST RATE	FEES AND CHANGES
Buy now, pay later			
Bank Credit Card of your choice			
Payday lender			
Pay in 4			

Case Study: Emily's Short-Term Loan Struggle

Emily is 19 years old and has just started working part-time at a café while studying at TAFE. She earns about $500 per week, but she doesn't always budget carefully.

THE SITUATION

One week, Emily's car breaks down, and she needs $800 for urgent repairs. She doesn't have savings, so she applies for a short-term loan online. The lender advertises "Fast Cash – No Credit Check."

Emily is approved the same day. She borrows $800 with the agreement to repay it in 4 weeks. The loan comes with:

- 20% establishment fee ($160)
- 4% monthly fee ($32)

This means that in 4 weeks, Emily must repay $992.

THE PROBLEM

Emily forgets that she also has rent, phone, and food costs due that week. She can't afford to pay back the $992 on time.

The lender adds:

- Late fee: $20
- Additional monthly fee if unpaid: another $32

Her debt grows to $1,044 after just 1 week overdue.

THE CONSEQUENCES

Emily has to borrow money from friends to cover her rent.

The stress of constant repayment reminders affects her study and work. By the time she finally clears the debt 3 months later, she has paid back over $1,150 – much more than the original $800 loan.

Module 4 Spending

Topic 15 Short Term Loans

Why did Emily choose a short-term loan instead of other options?

What risks are linked to loans with high fees and short repayment times?

What other choices could Emily have considered
(e.g., budgeting, saving, talking to her employer, asking family, using a no-interest loan
scheme)?

If you were Emily's friend, what advice would you give her for the future?

Summary Points

- When it comes to short-term loans they should be avoided where possible through good budgeting.
- Consider carefully before taking a short-term loan if the purchase is a need, a want, or if it can wait.

Topic 16

Rent or Purchase

Spectrum Debate

EITHER ON PAPER OR IN THE CLASSROOM, EVALUATE EACH OF THE FOLLOWING STATEMENTS USING THE RANGE STRONGLY DISAGREE, DISAGREE, NEUTRAL, AGREE, OR STRONGLY AGREE. BE READY TO JUSTIFY YOUR POSITION.

Learning Objective

By the end of this lesson students will be able to:

- Evaluate advantages and disadvantages of renting or purchasing products.
- Share a nuanced perspective, identifying times where it is better to rent or purchase

Key Terms

- Rent
- Share Economy

Owning your own home should still be the Great Australian Dream.

STRONGLY AGREE   AGREE   NEUTRAL   DISAGREE   STRONGLY DISAGREE

Renting a giant ladder from Bunnings is better than buying one for a task around the home.

STRONGLY AGREE   AGREE   NEUTRAL   DISAGREE   STRONGLY DISAGREE

Using Uber all the time is better than owning a car.

STRONGLY AGREE   AGREE   NEUTRAL   DISAGREE   STRONGLY DISAGREE

Hiring a green Lime bike works better than owning and using my own push bike.

STRONGLY AGREE   AGREE   NEUTRAL   DISAGREE   STRONGLY DISAGREE

Renting a dress or suit for the Year 12 Formal makes good sense.

STRONGLY AGREE   AGREE   NEUTRAL   DISAGREE   STRONGLY DISAGREE

Car share services are the way to go in a modern city; no one should own their own car.

STRONGLY AGREE   AGREE   NEUTRAL   DISAGREE   STRONGLY DISAGREE

If I owned a car, I would be keen to make it available to other people to drive through a car-sharing app.

STRONGLY AGREE   AGREE   NEUTRAL   DISAGREE   STRONGLY DISAGREE

When I use Uber, I like to choose the ride share option to reduce the cost and meet new people.

STRONGLY AGREE   AGREE   NEUTRAL   DISAGREE   STRONGLY DISAGREE

Module 4 Spending

Topic 16 Rent or Purchase

There is no correct answer when it comes to "Is owning or renting better?" It really comes down to context. There are a range of factors to consider, including:

- How often you will need the product?
- Cost of purchasing the product
- Cost of rental
- How often does the product need to be replaced/ does it wear out?
- Are there justifiable emotional factors in the decision e.g., I want to own my wedding dress and keep it even though I will only wear it once.
- Do I have space to store the product when it is not in use?
- How easy is it to access the rented product when I need it?

Rental costs typically allow for a percentage of the product cost plus profit margins for the renter. The cost will account for the ongoing maintenance of the product e.g., Airbnb includes cleaning fees as well as the normal costs of home ownership plus a profit.

Rental does not always mean you have the item at home. An example might be a home printer. You could purchase and maintain a home printer, or you could go to Officeworks to print jobs as needed. Similarly, you could purchase an exercise bike and weights for a home gym, or you could pay for a gym membership, which gives you access similar to renting.

THE FOLLOWING CHARACTERS HAVE DIFFERENT NEEDS AND WILL THEREFORE HAVE DIFFERENT RENTING AND BUYING PREFERENCES. READ THEIR CASE STUDY AND PROPOSE RENT OR BUY PREFERENCES ON THE NEXT PAGE.

Zara

- Apprentice Plumber.
- Uses a car for work.
- Lives in parents' large home in Western Sydney.

Leo

- Computing Engineer.
- Lives in a studio apartment in the Inner City.
- Tends to eat meals at work due to long hours.

Mia

- Primary School Teacher
- Works and lives in the same suburb
- Lives in a unit above a shopping complex.
- Enjoys beach getaways each school holiday.

Toby

- Training to become a nurse.
- Education expenses are tough when only earning a casual wage through bar work.
- Living in a shared unit near uni.

PERSON	ITEM	RENT / PAY PER USE	BUY / OWN
Zara 18	Car		
	Electric Tool Package		
	Printer		
	Treadmill for home gym		
Leo 17	Car		
	Electric Tool Package		
	Printer		
	Treadmill for home gym		
Mia 18	Car		
	Electric Tool Package		
	Printer		
	Treadmill for home gym		
Toby 17	Car		
	Electric Tool Package		
	Printer		
	Treadmill for home gym		

What surprises you?

What factors have the most impact?

Work   **Home**

Personal Preferences   **Finance**

Topic 16 Rent or Purchase

Cloud Computing is a form of rental. Rather than using hard drive space that you own, you pay a provider like Apple, Google, or Dropbox to store your files for you. Is Spotify similar, so you rent your music rather than buy vinyl or CDs?

Personal Reflection

What makes sense for you to rent or buy at this point in your life? Consider physical items as well as subscription services.

Summary Points

- When buying, always look for hidden costs and the total expense over time (e.g., maintenance, insurance).
- There will be situations where renting is better than buying and others where the opposite is true.

Topic 17

Subscription Services

Learning Objective

By the end of this lesson students will be able to:

- Identify strengths and challenges of subscription services.
- Evaluate the value of subscription vs outright ownership

Key Terms

- Subscription
- Rent
- Outright Purchase

Stock Take Time

Think about your whole household and write down subscription services that any member of your home has had previously, have currently got or would like to have in the future. Think about TV, Gaming, Phone, Gym, Ancestry, entertainment season passes, etc.

Services you have previously had

Services you currently have

Services you would like in the future

Topic 17 Subscription Services

It is easy to build a portfolio of video subscription services that are easy to sign up to and can add up financially. Research the cost and services offered by each provider and then put them in preference order based on your viewing interests.

SERVICE	MONTHLY COST	WHAT I LIKE ABOUT THIS SERVICE	PREFERENCE ORDER
Netflix			
Disney Plus			
Kayo			
Foxtel Now			
Binge			
Stan			
Apple TV+			
Prime Video			

Why is a Subscription Service useful?

What are reasons to avoid a Subscription Service?

Topic 17 Subscription Services

REFLECTING ON YOUR OWN LIFESTYLE AND PREDICTING THE NEXT 3 YEARS...

What services or products would be better as a subscription?

What services would be better to purchase outright?

Summary Points

· Review your subscriptions regularly; cancel services you don't use to save money.

· Use a calendar or reminder tool when you intend to cancel subscriptions. They often need to be cancelled several days before the new billing cycle.

Topic 18

Hidden Costs in Purchases

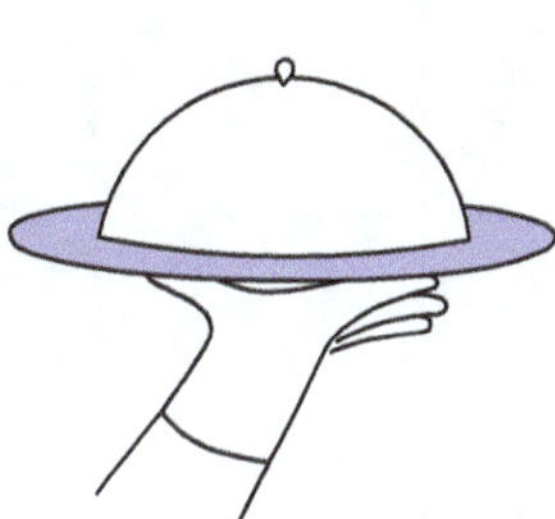

Learning Objective

By the end of this lesson students will be able to:

· Describe the difference between initial cost and total cost of ownership.

· Identify a range of hidden costs in regular transactions.

Key Terms

· Hidden Costs
· Total Cost of Ownership
· Transaction Fee

IDENTIFY HIDDEN COSTS FROM THE IMAGES ABOVE.

Topic 18 Hidden Costs in Purchases

Hidden costs are those that are not necessarily obvious but are a necessary part of the product or service. Purchasing a printer is a good example, the printer might cost a few hundred dollars but you also need replacement ink, paper and electricity.

COMPLETE THE FOLLOWING TABLE FOR **A NIGHT OUT AT THE MOVIES**.

ITEM OR SERVICE	COST	OBVIOUS OR HIDDEN
Movie Ticket	$18	Obvious
HIDDEN COSTS		
Popcorn and Drink		Hidden
Transport to and from		Hidden
Online Booking Fee		Hidden
Dinner before the movie		Hidden
Coffee or Snack after the movie		Hidden
Other?		Hidden
Total Cost		

COMPLETE THE FOLLOWING TABLE FOR **A DAY AT THE BEACH**.

ITEM OR SERVICE	COST	OBVIOUS OR HIDDEN
Swimming at the Beach	$0	Obvious
Total Cost		

ITEM OR SERVICE	COST	OBVIOUS OR HIDDEN
Total Cost		

HIDDEN COST	DESCRIPTION AND EXAMPLE
Card surcharges for tapping at a cash register.	
Withdrawing Money from a private ATM compared to one from your bank.	
Excess data usage charges on a phone plan.	
Fees for purchasing a product online in a foreign currency.	
Delivery costs for online shopping.	
Tips for wait staff at a restaurant.	
Ongoing consumables such as ink cartridges.	

Summary Points

- Financial charges can be avoided by choosing the correct ATM or options at an EFT terminal.
- When budgeting or considering a purchase, you should consider the total cost of ownership not just the initial outlay.

Topic 19

Accommodation

FIND 15 WORDS ASSOCIATED WITH ACCOMMODATION

```
R  E  N  T  A  L  A  G  R  E  E  M  E  N  T
A  T  N  E  D  E  P  E  D  N  I  R  S  T  U
W  D  E  P  O  S  I  T  A  L  H  U  A  O  E
E  V  C  V  O  S  P  R  N  E  D  I  C  H  G
K  I  D  M  D  T  E  E  U  L  D  B  C  N  E
I  L  O  I  E  A  U  L  A  V  S  E  A  O  N
N  L  S  N  A  Y  B  C  G  E  O  R  T  U  A
S  A  A  H  P  S  L  E  T  E  T  E  E  S  N
I  L  A  O  S  T  L  R  O  G  E  N  R  E  T
N  R  P  M  M  A  A  A  R  U  N  D  E  G  O
C  E  O  E  E  Y  R  S  E  A  D  T  C  A  R
E  N  A  A  N  T  L  N  P  A  E  O  T  G  E
X  E  T  N  E  T  N  A  D  R  A  L  L  H  T
L  S  H  A  R  E  H  O  U  S  E  N  M  R  P
S  T  U  D  I  O  F  L  A  T  N  S  T  R  W
```

Learning Objective

By the end of this lesson students will be able to:

- Define a range of terms associated with housing.
- Identify advantages and disadvantages of housing options

Key Terms

- Body Corporate
- Bond
- Strata
- Rental Agreement

In the Australian context there are two traditional approaches to accommodation. Either buying your own home or renting. The definition of home is a little more complex as it could include the obvious house or unit but there are many other accommodation approaches. This unit will explore traditional, emerging and unconventional approaches to living arrangements. Understanding the following terms is important background information.

TERM	DEFINITION
Rental	
Ownership	
Apartment	
Unit	
Strata	
Duplex	
Villa	
Body Corporate	
Bond	
Real-estate Agent	
Property Manager	
Conveyancer	
Mortgage	
University College	

Topic 19 Accommodation

No single accommodation type is perfect for everyone. Complete the following table identifying the advantages and disadvantages of each.

ACCOMMODATION	ADVANTAGES	DISADVANTAGES
Owning a house		
Owning a Unit		
Renting a House		
Renting a Unit		
Long-term Air BNB / Stayz		
Caravan or Motor Home		
Houseboat		
Retirement Village		
Bond		
Real-estate Agent		
Property Manager		
Conveyancer		
Mortgage		
University College		

Legislation changes regularly in the rental and housing domains. Choose one of the following topics to research. Summarise recent changes to legislation.

Topics include: No Grounds Eviction, Pets in Rental Accommodation, Proposals to Limit Airbnb rentals, and other topics agreed with your teacher.

Summary Points

- Housing is complex and differs greatly from city to city and country to country.
- Legislation and costs around housing change regularly, and you should seek independent advice before making big decisions.

Topic 20

Budgeting Priorities

Maya Case Study

Maya tossed her headphones onto her desk and leaned back, exhaling slowly. A large, empty spreadsheet titled "THE ADULT LIFE BUDGET" glared back at her from the laptop screen. Her summer job at the local library had been fun, but seeing that fat number in her savings account had hit differently. Now, her goal was a big one: saving for a six-month exchange program in Japan next year. The spreadsheet, however, felt like a quiz she hadn't studied for.

"Okay, let's start with the basics," she muttered, typing in a number under INCOME – her current savings, plus what she expects to earn over the next twelve months. Easy enough. Then came the hard part: EXPENSES. She instantly keyed in "$15/week" for her streaming services. Easy. Next, her friend Liam was saving up for a car, but Maya needed to save for the actual trip. That meant things like visa application fees and travel insurance. She scribbled those down on a notepad. She glanced at her empty water bottle. Last week, she'd bought three coffees and two expensive smoothies after school. She knew she had to factor in food and drinks, not just for school lunches, but those impulsive after-school purchases, too. Did she need a category for 'Fun Money' to prevent herself from constantly breaking the budget? Her phone buzzed – a text from her mum: "Need to order new running shoes for school athletics. Don't forget your replacements and repairs budget!" Ugh. She added Clothing/Footwear and a note about her phone screen, which was currently held together by a prayer and a cracked protector. The biggest

Learning Objective

By the end of this lesson students will be able to:

- Identify the range of priorities and how they fit into a budget.

Key Terms

- Needs
- Wants
- Budget
- Savings

mystery was the SINKING FUNDS. She knew this was for big, irregular things. Her family's holiday was coming up—she needed money for gifts and souvenirs (Gifts/Special Occasions). And what about the cost of getting to and from the library job? Bus tickets were a weekly thing (Transportation). Suddenly, the whole process felt less like a quiz and more like building a fortress, brick by financial brick. She realised a budget wasn't just about what she spent, but about priorities – how much of her money she was dedicating to her goal versus to her immediate needs and wants. Maya sighed, but this time, there was a tiny smile. The spreadsheet was still mostly empty, but the notepad was full of ideas. She now had categories that went way beyond rent and bills.

Needs:
The essentials

Wants:
The nice to haves

Needs and Wants are easy by idea, but where you draw the line between is a little trickier. For instance, it might be possible to walk to work, so catching a bus is a want. What happens if that walk is an hour? Alternatively, if public transport takes 2 hours, is it justifiable to say owning a car is a need rather than a want?

COMPLETE THE FOLLOWING TABLE USING MAYA'S CASE STUDY.

NEEDS	WANTS

NOW DO THE SAME FOR YOU.

NEEDS	WANTS

Topic 20 Budgeting Priorities

Now think about your Priorities for your own budget. List items on the left, followed by approximate price. You might also include how often you need to purchase (weekly, monthly, annually, etc). Try to include everything, such as birthday presents, social events, work equipment, clothing, transport, subscriptions, etc.

ITEM / CATEGORY	COST PER WEEK	PRIORITY (HIGH, MEDIUM, LOW)

RULE	EXPLANATION
50:30:20 Rule	Budget 50% of your income towards living expenses like rent, bills, and groceries. Budget 30% of your income towards lifestyle costs like eating out, new clothes, or concert tickets. Save the remaining 20% of your income.
70:20:10 Rule	The 70:20:10 rule is a budgeting system that divides your income into three categories: 70% for needs, 20% for wants, and 10% for savings.
Dave Ramsey Rules	Giving (10%), Saving (10%), Food (10% – 15%), Utilities (5% – 10%), Housing (25%), Transportation (10%).
The $27.40 Rule	The "$27.40 rule" is a daily savings strategy where you set aside $27.40 per day to save approximately $10,000 in a year.

The above rules demonstrate there is no one size fits all approach to budgeting. Everyone is different. However, it is important to have a budget, goals and balance both during school years and beyond. Some people even set up separate accounts for known bills and expenses while another account is for spending on incidentals.

Which of the above models fit you best? Why?

Summary Points

- A budget is a plan for your money—it tells every dollar where to go before you spend it.
- Needs and wants are both important but need to be in balance.
- There are many approaches to establishing your spending patterns but having no plan is a bad idea.

Topic 21

Budgeting Design

You have just received a surprise $1000 gift. Allocate that money across the following categories. You must use at least 3 fields and must use the full $1000.

ITEM	NEED (MUST HAVE FOR DAILY LIFE)	WANT (NICE TO HAVE)	GOAL (FUTURE/ LONG-TERM)	ALLOCATED AMOUNT ($)
New Phone (old one is broken)	○	○	○	
New Gaming Console	○	○	○	
Savings for a large future purchase (e.g., car, trip)	○	○	○	
Clothing for the current season	○	○	○	
Fuel/Bus Pass for the next month	○	○	○	
Tickets to a concert/festival	○	○	○	
Buying Lunch at school for two weeks	○	○	○	
Paying off a Debt to a friend/family member	○	○	○	

TOTAL
Must equal $1000

Learning Objective

By the end of this lesson students will be able to:

· Have developed understanding and skill sufficient to build a basic personal budget.

Key Terms

· Fixed expenses
· Variable expenses
· Net position

Now we will start constructing your own personal budget. There is a range of areas to consider.

Income

- Part-Time/Casual Job Pay
  (Net – After Tax)
- Allowance/Pocket Money
- Other Income (e.g. occasional jobs, birthday money)

The Future – Savings & Goals

SAVINGS GOALS

- **Short-Term Goal**
  (e.g. New Laptop, Concert Tickets, Clothing Item)
- **Long-Term Goal**
  (e.g. Trip to Japan, Car Fund, University/Housing Deposit)
- **Emergency Fund**
  (Money for unexpected problems – e.g. phone replacement)

Expenses

FIXED EXPENSES

- **Connectivity**
  Mobile Phone Bill, Internet Share (if applicable), Streaming Subscriptions (Netflix, Spotify, etc.)
- **Loan Repayments**
  Paying off money owed to a person or institution (e.g. student loan, phone payment plan)
- **Regular Fees**
  Gym Membership, Sports/Club Fees

VARIABLE EXPENSES

- **Food & Drink**
  School Canteen/Takeout, Groceries (if responsible for own snacks/lunch), Coffee/Treats
- **Transportation**
  Bus/Train Fares, Fuel/Petrol (if driving), Uber/Rideshare
- **Personal Care**
  Haircuts, Toiletries, Makeup/Grooming Products
- **Clothing & Shopping**
  New Clothes, Shoes, Accessories
- **Social & Entertainment**
  Movies, Dates/Outings, Video Games/In-Game Purchases
- **Gifts & Occasions**
  Birthdays, Christmas, Mother/Father's Day gifts
- **Miscellaneous/Buffer**
  Unexpected costs (e.g. lost equipment, small fees)
- **Donations/Charity**
  Any money set aside for giving

Topic 21 Budgeting Design

DOMAIN	ITEM	WEEKLY AMOUNT	MONTHLY AMOUNT	ANNUAL AMOUNT
Income	Part-Time Job			
	Allowances			
	Gifts and other occasional income			
Total				

FIXED EXPENSES

DOMAIN	ITEM	WEEKLY AMOUNT	MONTHLY AMOUNT	ANNUAL AMOUNT
Connectivity	Phone Bill			
	Internet Share			
	Streaming Subs			
	(Other)			
	(Other)			
Loan Repayments	(Specify)			
	(Specify)			
Regular Fees	Gym Membership			
	(Other)			
	(Other)			

VARIABLE EXPENSES

DOMAIN	ITEM	WEEKLY AMOUNT	MONTHLY AMOUNT	ANNUAL AMOUNT
Food & Drink	Canteen			
	Coffee & Drinks			
	Groceries			

DOMAIN	ITEM	WEEKLY AMOUNT	MONTHLY AMOUNT	ANNUAL AMOUNT
Transport	Public Transport			
	Uber			
	Car expenses			
Personal Care	Haircuts, nails, etc.			
Clothing	New clothes, shoes, accessories			
Social & Entertainment	Movies, Dates/Outings, Video Games/In-Game Purchases			
Gifts & Occasions	Birthdays, Christmas, Mother's/Father's Day gifts			
Miscellaneous / Buffer	Unexpected costs (e.g., lost equipment, small fees)			
Donations / Charity	Any money set aside for giving			
	Total Expenses			
	Total Income			
Saving Goals	Short, Medium & Long-Term Goals			
Net Position (Income – Expenses – Savings)				

Summary Points

- How closely does your draft budget align with your preferred model from the previous topic, e.g., 70:20:10?
- To balance a budget, you need to increase income, decrease spending, or both!

Module 4 Spending

Review

Glossary Terms

TERM	DEFINITION
Budget	A financial plan that projects and controls your income and expenses, ensuring you spend less than you earn.
Interest Rate	The cost a lender charges the borrower for the use of money, expressed as a percentage of the principal (or loan balance).
Mortgage	A very large, secured, long-term loan used specifically for the purchase of real estate (property).
Personal Loan	A medium-term, typically unsecured loan used for general purchases (like a car or holiday), often with a higher interest rate than a mortgage.
Hidden Costs	Unforeseen or less obvious expenses associated with a purchase, such as delivery fees, stamp duty, or ongoing maintenance.
Subscription	A recurring fee for ongoing access to a service (e.g., streaming, software); requires active management to avoid wasted money.
Secured Loan	A loan backed by an asset (like a house or car), which the lender can take if the borrower fails to repay the debt.
Unsecured Loan	A loan that is not backed by an asset, making it higher risk for the lender, resulting in higher interest rates.

Chapter Summary

This module provided practical strategies for controlling your outflows and mastering the essential skill of budgeting.

- **Cost of Borrowing:** You analysed how different types of loans, from short-term loans to credit cards, carry different interest rates, with lower-risk loans like mortgages typically having lower rates than personal loans.
- **Hidden Costs & Subscriptions:** You developed a critical eye for hidden expenses in major purchases and learned to regularly audit and cancel unnecessary subscription services to free up cash.
- **Rent vs. Buy:** We discussed the financial factors involved in deciding whether renting or purchasing an item (or accommodation) is the better economic choice in various situations.
- **Budgeting is Essential:** The core takeaway is that a budget is a forward-looking plan for your money, defining how much you will spend on categories like accommodation, food, and transport.
- **Budget Design:** You learned practical methods, such as the 70:20:10 rule (or similar models), to design a balanced budget that helps you increase your income or decrease your expenses.
- **Action Item:** Create a simple 30-day budget plan based on a fictional or real income source, using one of the budgeting models discussed.

Further Links

https://moneysmart.gov.au/budgeting/budget-planner

https://www.asic.gov.au/for-consumers/loans-and-credit-cards/

https://moneysmart.gov.au/other-ways-to-borrow/rent-vs-buy-calculator

Module 5

Investing

Learning Outcomes:

LO2

Analyse and evaluate financial products and services using critical thinking and cost-benefit analysis to make informed decisions.

LO3

Understand and exercise roles, rights, and responsibilities as consumers in both physical and digital environments.

Overview:

This module seeks to establish basic concepts and develop an understanding of how banks and government interact with individuals.

Topics:

Superannuation

Imagine yourself in retirement. Mind Map the activities you would like to be doing, places you would like to go, and things you would like to have.

Learning Objective

By the end of this lesson, students will be able to:

· Understand what superannuation is and its goals.

Key Terms

· Superannuation
· Retirement
· Risk Profile
· Investment Options

Module 5 Investing

Topic 22 Superannuation

What is Superannuation?

The Australian Superannuation System ("Super") is essentially a compulsory long-term savings plan for your retirement, designed so you can fund your own life after you stop working. When you get a job, your employer is legally required to pay a minimum percentage (currently 11%) of your wages into a special investment account, called a super fund, which is held in your name. This money is then invested by the fund managers in things like shares and property, allowing it to grow over many decades through compound interest, and you generally can't touch it until you retire, making it a powerful way to build a large financial safety net for your future self.

When you get a job, you need to provide your employer with your superannuation ('super') fund details. If you don't have one, your employer can help you with setting up their default super company. Super funds are just like health insurance, where there are lots of providers that offer similar products with different costs, inclusions, and exclusions. To put it more simply, it's a bit like the takeaway food industry – there are many options for dinner; they have different levels of service, inclusions, quality, etc. What suits you is not necessarily right for the next person. The following table is a general summary of the types of products a typical super fund offers.

OPTION TYPE	RISK PROFILE	FOCUS (ASSET ALLOCATION)	TYPICAL INVESTOR
High Growth	High	Heavily weighted towards growth assets (e.g., 80-90% shares/property).	Younger people with a long time until retirement who can tolerate market ups and downs.
Growth	Medium-High	Strong bias toward growth assets (e.g., 70-80% shares/property).	Members with still a significant time from retirement.
Balanced	Medium	A mix, often with a slight bias to growth (e.g., 60-75% growth assets).	Suits most people aiming for long-term growth with some stability. It's the most common default.
Conservative	Medium-Low	More defensive assets than growth (e.g., 50% or more cash / fixed interest).	People closer to retirement who want to protect their savings.
Cash	Very Low	Almost entirely in cash and short-term deposits.	Very low-risk option, but returns are typically the lowest.

You will find that all superannuation funds advertise "past performance is no guarantee of future results". By this, what they mean is that you should look to see how they have performed historically, it is essentially their report card. However, just because a previous report was good or bad, it does not necessarily mean the next one will be similar.

When you look at the following graph, you will see that some investment types do not always grow. Sometimes the stock market makes a loss, sometimes the value of the Australian Dollar drops or rises, sometimes the price of oil goes up or down; these variations impact your investments.

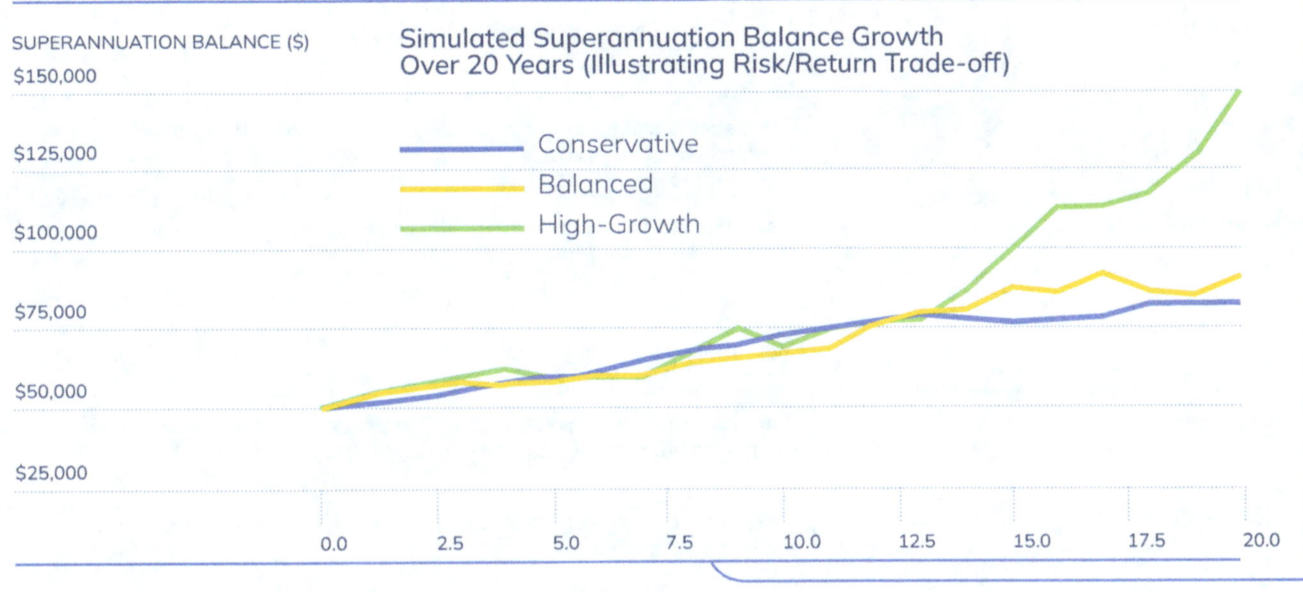

QUESTION	ANSWER
Which investment option is best after 20 years?	
Which investment option is best after 10 years?	
Which investment option is best after 4 years?	
What happens to the balanced option between years 17 and 19?	
In what years does High Growth experience the most loss?	

Topic 22 Superannuation

MATCH THE TERM TO ITS DEFINITION

Term		Definition
Investment Option		The stage of life when you stop working for good.
Fees and Charges		Extra services like income protection or death cover that are often bundled with your super.
Performance		How well the fund's investments have grown over many years compared to other funds.
Insurance		What the fund charges you to manage your money. Lower fees mean more money stays in your account.
Retirement		How your money is invested (e.g., Shares, Property). Growth options are riskier but aim for higher returns over the long term.
Employer Contributions		The percentage of your pay that your employer is legally required to put into your super.
Super Fund		A company that manages and invests your super money.
Superannuation Guarantee		The money your boss must pay into your super fund.

Summary Points

- Super is your retirement money. It's locked away until you retire, but it's crucial for your future financial security.
- Super is paid by your employer into your chosen account.

Shares

Shares are a way of owning a small amount of a business. When you buy shares, you take the risk of losses and the opportunities of profits just as the business itself does. To start this topic, review the following 3 businesses and complete the table underneath, selecting where you would like to invest a fictitious $100.

Green Wave Energy

Sells affordable home solar panels and battery storage. Strong environmental focus. e.g. phone replacement)

Steady Foods Inc

Owns a reliable chain of essential supermarkets and distribution warehouses.

Next Gen Gaming

Develops and sells popular, but expensive, new video game consoles and VR headsets

Learning Objective

By the end of this lesson, students will be able to:

· Describe shares as an investment option.

Key Terms

· Share
· Stock Market
· Dividend
· Equity

COMPANY	$ AMOUNT INVESTED	REASON FOR THIS ALLOCATION
GreenWave Energy	$	
Steady Foods Inc.	$	
NextGen Gaming	$	
TOTAL	$100	

THE DAILY INVESTOR NEWS

MARKET WATCH: MID -DAY REPORT
Key Market Movers

SOLAR SURGE! Tax Rebate Fuels Massive Gains

Shares in GreenWave Energy, the leading provider of affordable solar panels and home battery units, rocketed up 80% this morning. The sudden jump was triggered by a government announcement of a new, generous national tax rebate for all household renewable energy installations. Analysts project this policy will create a sudden, massive spike in consumer demand, potentially doubling GreenWave's order backlog and future profits. Investors are now scrambling to buy in, betting heavily on the high-growth potential of the clean energy sector.

UP 80% FROM $1.00 TO $1.80

Steady Foods Holds Line as Sector Remains Stable

The stock for supermarket giant Steady Foods Inc. saw a modest, predictable increase following the release of its quarterly sales report. The company, known for its essential grocery chains and reliable distribution network, announced figures that met all market expectations but showed no significant acceleration. Investors view this as a positive sign of stability and low risk, particularly during periods of economic uncertainty. This predictable, non-volatile stock appeals primarily to cautious investors seeking slow, dependable returns.

UP 10% FROM $1.00 TO $1.10

Chip Shortage Panic! Gaming Shares Plummet

NextGen Gaming, the innovative console developer, saw its share price collapse by 60% after issuing a shock profit warning. The company confirmed that a severe global shortage of essential microchips will force them to delay the launch of their highly anticipated new console by six months. This news has triggered immediate panic selling, as the delay means a complete loss of crucial holiday sales revenue. The value reflects the immediate risk and loss of investor confidence in the company's ability to deliver its product.

DOWN 60% FROM $1.00 TO $0.40

STOCK	INITIAL INVESTMENT FROM INITIAL TABLE	MARKET CHANGE	NEW VALUE
GreenWave Energy	$	Up 80% Initial Investment x1.8	
Steady Foods Inc.	$	Up 80% Initial Investment x1.8	
NextGen Gaming	$	Down 80% Initial Investment x 0.4	

Shares are a way of owning a small amount of a business.
When you buy shares, you take the risk of losses and the
opportunities of profits just as the business itself does.
To start this topic, review the following 3 businesses and
complete the table underneath, selecting where you
would like to invest a fictitious $100.

THE DAILY INVESTOR NEWS

MARKET WATCH: MID -DAY REPORT
Key Market Movers

SOLAR SURGE but no Christmas Bonus for Investors

Shares in GreenWave have risen this year, however, the board has chosen to reinvest profits in new equipment. No dividends in sight.

DIVIDEND PAYOUT $0

Steady Foods Helps investors with Modest Dividend

A 10 cent per share dividend has been issued by the board.

DIVIDEND PAYOUT $0.10

Just like their explosive product range Investors win big

Despite plummeting share prices, the board is issuing a massive $1.10 dividend for each share!

DIVIDEND PAYOUT $1.10

Module 5 Investing

Topic 23 Shares

STOCK	INITIAL INVESTMENT FROM INITIAL TABLE	CURRENT VALUE CALCULATED ON PREVIOUS PAGE	ADD DIVIDEND BASED ON THE INITIAL NUMBER OF SHARES PURCHASED (THEY WERE $1 EACH)	FINAL VALUE OF SHARES PLUS ANY DIVIDENDS
GreenWave Energy				
Steady Foods Inc.				
NextGen Gaming				

The example from this unit shows how market fluctuations move the value of your investment. Share values move up and down based on a huge range of factors, and ultimately, market confidence. Things like a country's employment levels, inflation, the value of the currency, and international factors like changing trade or war all influence the value of shares. In addition to the cost of shares themselves, there are also management fees, such as a broker's costs or

in the case of online transactions, the platform might charge a fee either outright as a dollar amount or as a percentage. It is possible to either invest in shares directly, where you select a share and purchase it through a broker or platform. Alternatively, you can invest in shares through a company that manages shares on your behalf, and you simply indicate how aggressively or safely you wish to invest, and they trade shares on your behalf for a fee.

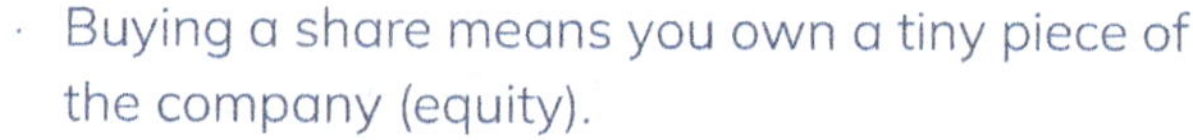

Summary Points

- Buying a share means you own a tiny piece of the company (equity).
- You make money from shares through dividends and when the share price increases.

Emerging Investments

HISTORICAL CURRENCY	WHAT MAKES IT VALUABLE?
Cowrie Shells: One of the most widely and longest-used forms of currency, particularly in parts of Africa, Asia, and Oceania, dating back to ancient China.	
Whale Teeth: Used as a valuable currency, known as 'tabua', in Fiji.	
Salt: Historically very valuable due to its use as a food preservative and seasoning. The word "salary" is derived from the Latin word for salt (sal), referencing the idea of being paid in it (though the Roman connection is debated, salt was certainly a key medium of exchange).	
Tea Bricks: Compressed bricks of tea leaves used for trade in parts of China, Tibet, Mongolia, and Siberia.	
Precious Metals (Gold & Silver): Initially traded as weighed bars or lumps, which evolved into standardised coins.	
Paper Money (Banknotes): First developed in China during the Song Dynasty (around 7th to 11th century CE) as receipts for depositing metal coinage, later evolving into government-issued currency.	
Credit/Debit: A promise of value backed by a bank or financial institution, which has become the primary form of transaction in modern times.	
Digital/Cryptocurrency: A modern, decentralised form of currency based on digital records and cryptography, such as Bitcoin and Ethereum.	

Learning Objective

By the end of this lesson students will be able to:

- Outline the essential elements of cryptocurrency.
- Identify its opportunities and risks.

Key Terms

- Cryptocurrency
- NFT
- Blockchain

What is the Difference between Crypto-Currency and Bitcoin?

Crypto-Currency is an overarching term to reference a range of blockchain-based payment methods. Bitcoin is just one example of a Crypto-Currency, along with others such as Ethereum, Dogecoin, etc.

How does it work?

The Reserve Bank of Australia (RBA) explains the concepts in detail through the following site:

https://www.rba.gov.au/education/resources/explainers/cryptocurrencies.html

The following diagram comes from the RBA site and provides a step-by-step of how funds move from Alice to Bob.

There is a range of good videos that can be useful in further understanding the concept. Some include:

https://www.youtube.com/watch?v=-1ErJsH73Lk or https://www.youtube.com/watch?v=s4g1XFU8Gto

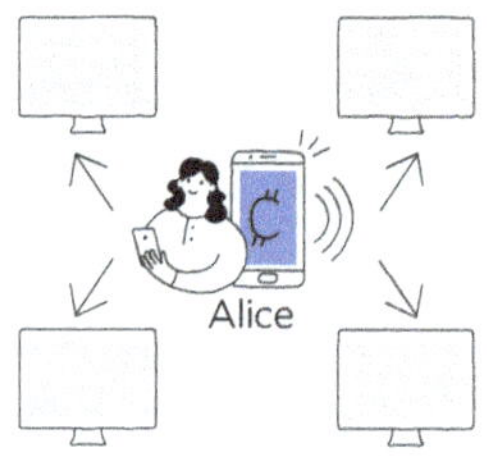

1

Alice sends instructions to transfer crypto-currency to Bob. **Anyone** using the **network** can view the message.

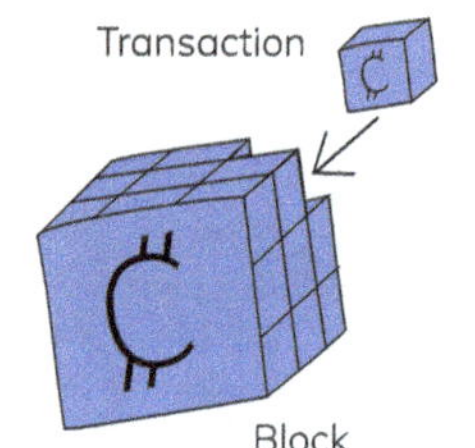

2

Miners group the transactions together into a 'block' with other recently sent transactions.

3

Information from the new block is transformed into a cryptographic **code**.

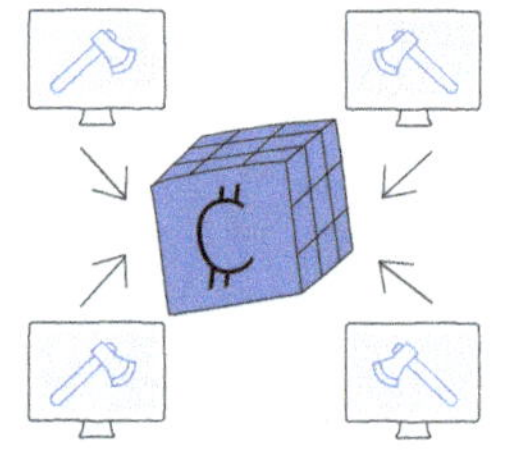

4

Miners **compete** to find the **code** that will add the new block to the blockchain.

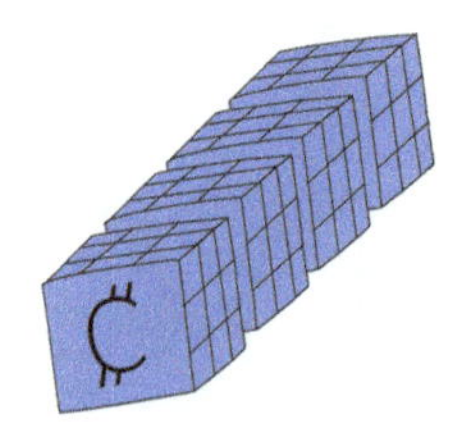

5

Once the code is solved, the block is added to the blockchain, and the transaction is confirmed.

6

Bob receives the cryptocurrency.

Features of the Bitcoin System

The most well-known crypto-currency is Bitcoin. Bitcoin was launched in 2009, a year after a report that described the Bitcoin system was released under the name Satoshi Nakamoto. The system was designed to electronically mimic features of a cash transaction. It was designed to allow peer-to-peer (or person-to-person) transactions, without the need to know
or trust the other person in the transaction, and to occur without the need for a central party (such as a bank). Unlike conventional national currencies such as Australian dollars, which get part of their value from being legislated as legal tender, Bitcoin and other crypto-currencies do not have any legislated or intrinsic value. Instead, the value of Bitcoin is determined by what people are willing to pay for it in the market (and, in theory, its value could fall to zero at any time).

One feature of the Bitcoin system is that the supply of Bitcoins increases at a pre-determined rate and is capped at around 21 million (with each bitcoin able to be subdivided into 100 million satoshis or 0.00000001 Bitcoins). Because of this, the supply of Bitcoins has been commonly compared to the supply of a scarce commodity, such as gold.

The Bitcoin system allows transactions to occur directly from person to person without requiring a central party (such as a bank) to verify or record the transactions. This is unlike most conventional payment methods, such as electronic bank transfers, which rely on a central party to keep and update records of transactions. For example, commercial banks maintain a record of their customers' account balances, deposits, and withdrawals.

Instead, the Bitcoin system uses 'blockchain' technology to record transactions and the ownership of Bitcoins. This is essentially technology that connects groups of transactions ('blocks') together over time
(in a 'chain'). Each time a transaction occurs, it forms part of a new block that is added to the chain. As a result, the blockchain provides a record (or database) of every Bitcoin transaction that has ever occurred, and it is available for anyone to access and update on a public network (this is often referred to as a 'distributed ledger'). The integrity of the Bitcoin system is protected by 'cryptography', which is a method of verifying and securing data using complex mathematical algorithms (or codes). This mak es the system very difficult to corrupt.

Bitcoin transactions are verified by other users of the network, and the process of compiling, verifying, and confirming transactions is often referred to as 'mining'. Specifically, complex codes need to be solved to confirm transactions and make sure the system is not corrupted. The Bitcoin system increases the complexity of these codes as more computing power is used to solve them. A new block of transactions is compiled approximately every ten minutes. 'Miners' want to solve the codes and process transactions because they are rewarded with new Bitcoins (currently 6.25 new Bitcoins per block).

The increase in competition between miners for new Bitcoins has seen large increases in the amount of computing power and electricity required (which is often used for air conditioning to cool computer systems). While it is dif ficult to calculate with precision, some estimates suggest that the annual energy consumption of the Bitcoin system is roughly equal to that of country of Thailand.

Module 5 Investing

Topic 24 Emerging Investments

What are the advantages of Crypto Currencies such as Bitcoin?

What are the disadvantages of Crypto-Currencies such as Bitcoin?

Would you invest in Bitcoin Today? Why or Why not?

Summary Points

- Be aware that new investments like cryptocurrency are often high-risk and volatile.
- Just like any investment, crypto can be a profit or loss-making venture.

Loyalty Reward Schemes

BRAINSTORM ALL THE BUSINESSES THAT YOU HAVE LOYALTY CARDS WITH, EXAMPLES COULD INCLUDE THE MCDONALDS APP, FLYBUYS OR COTTON ON.

Learning Objective

By the end of this lesson students will be able to:

- Describe the features of loyalty schemes.
- Evaluate the costs and benefits of programs that they currently use.

Key Terms

- Loyalty
- Reward Points
- Data Breach

"If you aren't paying for the product, you are the product."

What could this mean in terms of loyalty programs where you get something for nothing?

Module 5 Investing

Topic 25 Loyalty Reward Schemes

Read the following news article from ABC News on the Australian Competition and Consumer Commission (ACCC) report into loyalty programs:

https://www.abc.net.au/news/2025-03-22/accc-inquiry-supermarket-loyalty-programs/105081258

A screenshot of the article here gives a snapshot of what the Australian Competition and Consumer Commission found.

The "gamification" of supermarket loyalty programs could be influencing customers without them realising, according to the Australian Competition and Consumer Commission (ACCC).

On Friday, the ACCC released its final 441-page report from its inquiry into supermarkets across Australia, detailing the impact of loyalty programs on consumers.

Part of the report noted customers would need to spend thousands of dollars in stores to get a discount of just $10.

Woolies and Coles have 'limited incentive' to compete hard on price, ACCC finds

The consumer watchdog stops short of declaring grocery prices excessive.

The report recommended Coles and Woolworths be required to provide loyalty program members with "simple, plain-English" disclosure summaries to outline the monetary value of the program.

"The number of shoppers using the loyalty programs offered through Coles and Woolworths is growing," the report said.

"Loyalty programs generally have evolved from being merely rewards-based marketing tactics to being 'sophisticated data, marketing and customer engagement powerhouses.'"

———

CATEGORY	BRAND	WHAT DO YOU NEED TO SPEND TO GET A $10 BENEFIT? ARE THERE SETUP COSTS?	HOW EASY IS IT TO FIND INFORMATION ABOUT COSTS AND BENEFITS?
Finance	American Express		
Travel	QANTAS Frequent Flyer		
Retail	Flybuys		
	Everyday Rewards		
	My Maccas App		
	Cotton On Perks		
	EB Games		

Why would any of the above companies give away "free" benefits? What is in it for them?

Module 5 Investing

Topic 25 Loyalty Reward Schemes

Why are your shopping habits useful to retailers?

How do they use the data?

What could be the impact of data breaches on databases for loyalty programs?

How comfortable are you providing personal information to retailers for reward programs including your name, email, date of birth, etc.

Summary Points

- Use loyalty schemes strategically to save money, but don't let them trick you into overspending to earn points.
- Your data is valuable, make sure you trust companies before giving it out.

Scams

The following questions relate to Australian data from January to June 2025.

QUESTION	CIRCLE THE OPTION YOU THINK IS CORRECT		
The number of reported scams...	Decreased 24%.	Remained roughly stable.	Increased 63%.
The amount of financial losses to scams was $174m, which was...	A decrease of 71% from the same time last year.	Roughly similar to the previous year.	An increase of 26% from the same time last year
The average losses per scam were around A$12,212, which was...	A decrease of 10%.	Roughly similar to last year.	An increase of 10%.
The demographic that lost the most to scams...	Younger Australians	Middle Aged Australians	Older Australians
The demographic most likely to report a scam is...	Younger Australians	Middle Aged Australians	Older Australians
Rank the following groups in order from 1 – 3, where 1 experienced the biggest increase in losses...	People who have English as a Second Language	Computer Engineers	Indigenous Australians

Learning Objective

By the end of this lesson students will be able to:

- Describe a range of scams and the objectives of scammers.
- Recommend good habits to avoid being scammed.

Key Terms

- Scam
- Phishing
- Identity Theft

Module 5 Investing

Topic 26 Scams

In the first half of 2025, Australia saw a 24% decrease in scam reports but a 26% increase in total financial losses, reaching approximately $174 million. Investment and phishing scams were major contributors to losses, which were also driven by more sophisticated methods like AI-driven scams, crypto impersonation, and social media fraud. While older Australians continue to report the highest total losses, younger age groups report scams more frequently.

KEY STATISTICS FOR 2025 (FIRST SIX MONTHS)

- **Reports:**
  108,305 reports received, a 24% decrease from the same period in 2024.

- **Financial losses:**
  Approximately $174 million reported lost, a 26% increase from the first half of 2024.

- **Average loss:**
  The average reported loss was around $12,212, down about 10%.

MAJOR SCAM TYPES AND TRENDS

- **Investment scams:**
  Remain the leading cause of financial loss, though losses decreased slightly in early 2025.

- **Phishing and crypto scams:**
  Losses from phishing rose significantly, partly due to a surge in crypto impersonation scams.

- **Social media scams:**
  A 50% increase in reported losses through social media, totalling $23.4 million in the first half of the year.

- **AI and sophisticated scams:**
  Scammers are increasingly using AI for deepfakes and voice cloning, and sophisticated methods to impersonate brands and government agencies, such as a recent ATO impersonation email scam.

- **Identity theft:**
  There is an increase in the trading of stolen identities (passports, driver's licenses) on the dark web.

DEMOGRAPHICS MOST AFFECTED

- **By total loss:**
  Older Australians (65 and over) reported the highest total losses.

- **By reporting frequency:**
  Younger Australians (18-44) are the most likely to report experiencing a scam.

- **By increasing losses:**
  Financial losses to scams have increased significantly for individuals who speak English as a second language (44%) and for First Nations Australians (55.3%) compared to the same period in 2024.

SCAM TYPE	DESCRIBE IN GENERAL TERMS HOW IT WORKS AND WHAT SCAMMERS ARE LOOKING TO ACHIEVE.
Invoice Fraud	
Phishing	
Remote Access Scams	
Identity Theft	
Threats and Extortion	
Dating and Romance Scams	
Investment and Cryptocurrency Scams	

The following site will be useful in your research

https://www.cyber.gov.au/learn-basics/watch-out-threats/types-scams

Module 5 Investing

Topic 26 Scams

Create a tips guide for a teenager with your top 3 tips to avoid scams, or what to do if you are worried you have been scammed. Put your tip in the coloured box and explain more details in the white box immediately under.

TIP 1

TIP 2

TIP 3

Review

Glossary Terms

TERM	DEFINITION
Superannuation (Super)	Mandatory retirement savings in Australia; a percentage of your salary is paid by your employer into a super fund.
Shares	Units of ownership (equity) in a publicly listed company; buying them allows you to benefit from the company profits.
Dividend	A payment of a company's profit that is regularly distributed to its shareholders.
Cryptocurrency (Crypto)	A decentralised digital currency (e.g., Bitcoin); highly volatile and often considered a high-risk emerging investment.
Scam	A fraudulent scheme designed to trick people into giving away money, bank details, or personal identifying information.
ASIC	Australian Securities and Investments Commission; the government body responsible for regulating financial markets and protecting consumers from fraud.
Diversification	The strategy of investing in a variety of different assets (e.g., shares, property, cash) to reduce overall risk.
Risk	The potential for an investment's actual return to be different from the expected return; generally, higher risk means higher potential return, or loss.

Summary Points

- If an investment opportunity seems too good to be true, it's almost certainly a scam.
- Scams constantly evolve, so you should keep updated on emerging trends and risks.

Module 5 Investing

Chapter Summary

This module introduced you to making your money work for you, securing your retirement, and being aware of risks.

- Superannuation: You learned the importance of superannuation in the Australian system, which is mandatory savings for your retirement, and your employer is legally required to contribute to it.
- Shares: We defined shares as an investment, representing equity (ownership) in a company, and discussed the two ways to earn from them: dividends and capital gains (when the share price rises).
- New Risks: The module explored emerging investments like cryptocurrency, noting that while they may offer high returns, they are typically high-risk and volatile.
- Loyalty Schemes: You examined how loyalty and reward schemes work, emphasising the need to use them strategically for savings rather than letting them encourage unnecessary spending.
- Scam Awareness: You were given essential tips on how to identify and avoid common financial scams, reinforcing the principle that if an investment promises returns that are "too good to be true," it is likely a scam.
- Action Item: Research the current rate of the Superannuation Guarantee (SG) and check your understanding of when you can access your super.

Further Links

https://moneysmart.gov.au/how-super-works

https://moneysmart.gov.au/how-to-invest

https://moneysmart.gov.au/financial-scams/investment-scams

Major Project

Learning Outcomes:

LO1

Demonstrate personal financial management skills by applying knowledge of budgeting, saving, earning, and spending to real-world scenarios.

LO2

Analyse and evaluate financial products and services using critical thinking and cost-benefit analysis to make informed decisions.

LO3

Understand and exercise roles, rights and responsibilities as consumers in both physical and digital environments.

Overview:

Topics 27 – 31 provide you with 5 hours to pursue a major project of your choice. These options are some areas you could explore but the objective is to develop one or several of the following tools to support you into the future or to demonstrate the depth of your learning.

Options:

Review Financial Influencers

Develop own small business based on interests

Apply for employment

Record video explaining one of the above themes to peers for social media

Design future education plan

ASX Stock Market Game

Personal Priorities and Financial Future Plan (budget, aspirations, etc)

Other as approved by your teacher

Review of Financial Influencers

There is a huge range of financial influencers (finfluencers) online today. Using appropriate platforms of your, choice watch a range of influencers and capture their key messages. After reviewing a few different influencers, try to create a summary list of their common messages. You are encouraged to find your own influencers, but a starting point might include: Alan Kohler, Mark Bouris, or Vivian Tu.

NAME AND LINK	KEY MESSAGES	WHAT DO I LIKE?	WHAT AM I NOT SO SURE ABOUT?

Option 2

Design Your Own Business

If you are interested in starting your own small business or side hustle, take this as an opportunity to design it properly. The following dot points are designed to prompt your thinking about a range of considerations. Start a document where you plan out what you need to make this venture a success.

IDEA AND VALIDATION

- **Identify your skills and passions:** What are you good at? What do you enjoy doing?
- **Define your product or service:** What exactly are you offering?
- **Identify your target market:** Who will buy what you're selling? Be specific.
- **Validate your idea:** Is there a real demand for your product/service? (e.g., talk to potential customers, run a small test).
- **Assess the competition:** Who else is doing this? How will you differentiate yourself?

TIME AND CAPACITY

- **Determine available time:** How many hours per week can you realistically dedicate without burning out or compromising your main job/life?
- **Set realistic goals:** What do you want to achieve in the first 3, 6, and 12 months?
- **Establish boundaries:** How will you separate your side hustle time from your main job and personal life?
- **Plan for scalability:** Is your business model something you can easily manage when demand increases?

FINANCIALS

- **Calculate start-up costs:** What essential equipment, materials, or initial marketing expenses do you need?
- **Determine pricing:** How will you price your offering to cover costs and make a profit? (Don't forget to factor in your time!)
- **Create a basic budget/projections:** Estimate your expected income and expenses for the first year.
- **Track all income and expenses:** Set up a simple system (spreadsheet or app) from day one for tax purposes.
- **Decide how to handle profits:** Will you reinvest them, save them, or pay yourself?

LEGAL & ADMINISTRATIVE

- **Check legal/regulatory requirements:** Do you need a specific license, permit, or certification to operate in your area?
- **Choose a business structure:** Will you operate as a sole trader/proprietor, partnership, or Pty Ltd (check local requirements)?
- **Register your business name (if needed):** Check for availability and register it legally.
- **Understand your tax obligations:** What taxes (e.g., income tax, sales tax/GST) apply to your business earnings? (It's often wise to consult an accountant).
- **Look into insurance:** Do you need public liability or professional indemnity insurance?

MARKETING & OPERATIONS

- **Develop a simple brand:** A name, logo, and consistent voice.
- **Choose your platform:** Will you use a website, social media, an online marketplace (e.g., Etsy), or local markets?
- **Plan your customer experience:** How will you handle sales, delivery/fulfillment, and customer service?
- **Create a marketing strategy:** How will people find out about you? (e.g., word-of-mouth, social media content, paid ads).
- **Establish efficient processes:** How will you manage orders, inventory, invoicing, etc., to minimize time spent on admin?

Option 3

Apply for Employment

To apply, you need to consider:

· Where am I going to apply to? You will need to apply multiple times, as it is rare for someone to get their ideal job with their first application.

· What is the employer looking for in me?

· Draft a cover letter and resume or CV.

· Get a trusted adult to proofread your work – don't submit something with obvious spelling or grammatical errors.

· How do I submit the application – in person or online? Is there value in trying to meet the manager in person and hand your application to them to make a good impression?

· Prepare for an interview – search online for likely questions and rehearse your responses out loud with an experienced adult.

· What will you wear to an interview?

· What questions might you take to the interview that would leave a good impression?

Services Australia provide some great resources to consider as you begin looking for a job

https://www.servicesaustralia.gov.au/looking-for-work-and-job-hunting?context=60070

Video

Record a video explaining one of the above themes to peers for social media

Finfluencers are often pitched at economic or financial professionals, or alternatively, they are recorded for adults looking at major decisions like home ownership. There is a gap in the social media market for teens explaining complex financial concepts to other teens. Take this as your opportunity to start a social media presence to explain some of the concepts in this course.

Things to consider:

· Audience

· Duration

· Style

· Graphics

· Recording tools

· Editing tools

· Location, setting & lighting

· Platforms that can be monetised

· What impact will the Australian social media ban have on your target audience?

Before production, look at Option 1 in this module. What do those social media producers do that you like and would like to replicate? What do they do that you want to avoid?

Option 5

Design Future Education Plan

Before designing your learning plan, consider:

- What are my learning goals?
- Would I like to gain a good broad understanding of lots of things, or would I prefer to know a lot more about some favourite topics?
- How might my learning now help me in the future with my own finances or in securing work?
- How much money am I prepared to invest in my learning?
- When will I work on this learning?

Education is a lifelong exercise. Even those with Doctoral level degrees in Finance continue to seek out new learning especially with the rapid pace of change today. Fifteen years ago, the idea of Bitcoin and NFTs didn't exist and now they have disrupted the market. The ability to learn about traditional and emerging financial issues has become easier with the emergency of Massive Open Online Courses (MOOCs) and Micro Credentials. The following image is just one example of a course that you could choose to complete to continue expanding your understanding of finance.

What Is NFT Art? (How Does It Work)

Written by Coursera Staff • Updated on Jul 9, 2025   Share

As the metaverse continues to grow, learn about what non-fungible tokens (NFTs) are, how to create them, and ways to earn money selling them. Explore the NFT selling options for digital artwork and how you can get started in this developing field.

Non-fungible token (NFT) art refers to digital assets stored on a blockchain that represent content or even physical items. Art mediums that NFTs can represent include digital drawings, paintings, music, film, poetry, or books. NFT art allows artists to sell or rent their artwork beyond the physical world. Explore NFT art and how you can get involved in the NFT market.

QUESTION	ANSWER
What topics do I want to study next?	
What is the duration of this plan?	
Insert links or course names that I would like to study next.	
How will I hold myself accountable?	

Option 6

ASX Share Market Game

The Australian Stock Exchange (ASX) has run the Share Market Game for many years. It challenges you to use a fictitious amount of money and invest in the stock market. The aim of the game is simple – make as much money as you can. They typically run the competition twice each year, and it runs for a few months at a time.

Further details and dates are available at:
https://www.asx.com.au/investors/investment-tools-and-resources/sharemarket-game

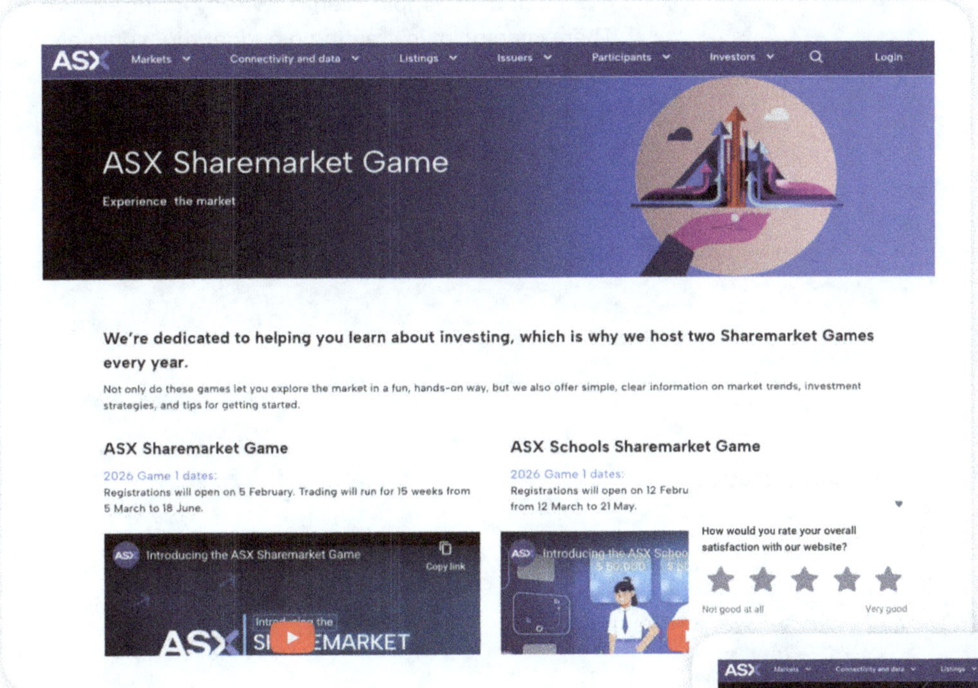

In addition to the game, they have a range of online learning courses:
https://www.asx.com.au/investors/investment-tools-and-resources/online-courses

These courses are a great way to understand topics including shares, EFTs, Bonds, Warrants and ASX listing rules.

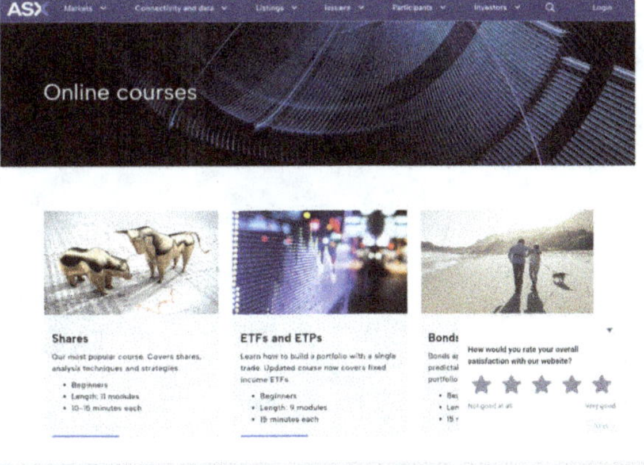

Personal Priorities and Financial Future Plan

(budget, aspirations, etc)

There is a huge range of budget tools available online. One of the best free options comes through the Australian Government Money Smart website:

https://moneysmart.gov.au/budgeting/budget-planner

What is good about this tool is that it has a huge range of categories for income, and expenses and you can categorise elements as weekly, fortnightly, monthly, or annually. In this way you can construct a budget that suits you and your lifestyle.

As you develop your budget, you need to be real. Honesty in budgeting is key. If you know you will buy a drink at the shopping centre, weekly include it. There is no point in creating a budget that could at best be considered creative writing.

As you sit with a budget, you should realise that it will change over time, and constantly be adjusted as income, expenses and goals in your life change.

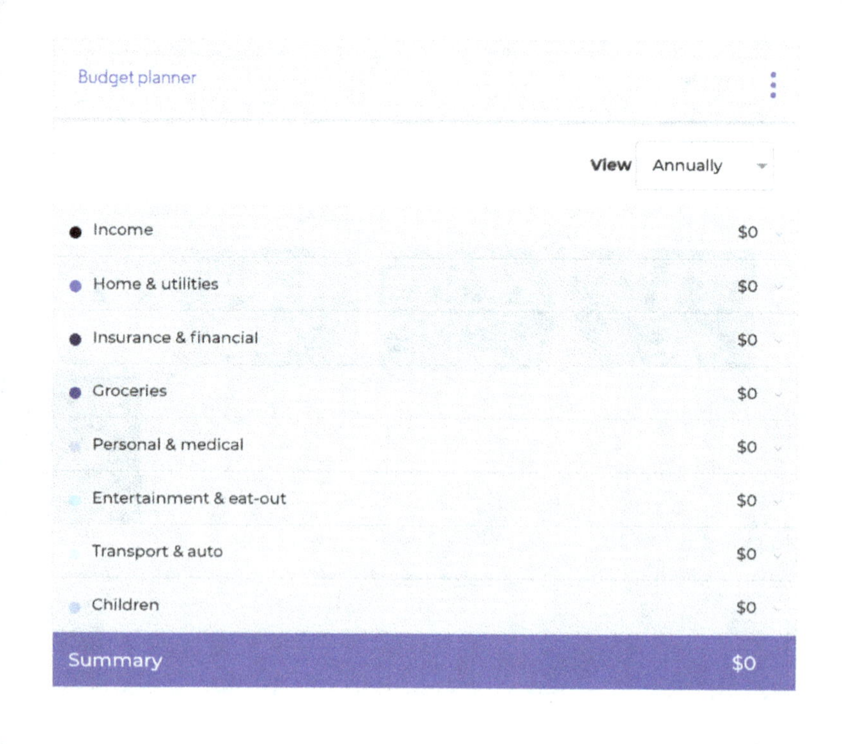

Setup

Learning Outcomes:

LO2

Analyse and evaluate financial products and services using critical thinking and cost-benefit analysis to make informed decisions.

LO4

Communicate financial ideas and decisions effectively using appropriate terminology, digital tools, and data representations.

Overview:

To conclude the course, you are now challenged to return to the concept of setup with a vision for the future. This module explores the next available steps in your educational journey regarding Financial Success.

Topics:

Module 7 Setup

Topic 28

Ongoing Education

TOPIC	PRIOR KNOWLEDGE	CURRENT KNOWLEDGE	DESIRE FOR MORE INFO
Understanding types of bank accounts			
How to engage with the Government			
Tax			
Credit Scores			
Compound Interest			
Borrowing Money			
Subscription Services vs Outright Purchase			
Budgeting			
Superannuation			
Shares			
Emerging Investments (Crypto Currency)			

Learning Objective

By the end of this lesson, students will be able to:

· Describe sources of good and poor financial advice.

Key Terms

· Micro Credential
· Life Long Learning

Lifelong learning is a reality in almost every workplace and every aspect of your future. As the world changes, you need to keep abreast of what is changing to best support yourself financially. A good example of this is the introduction of cryptocurrencies, something that simply did not exist when your parents were at school. Aside from the big disruptive changes like crypto there are smaller constant changes like taxation law or government benefits that you may be able to access.

There are government and not-for-profit organisations that can be useful places to continue your learning in financial literacy. A good example is the Ecstra Foundation. Take a look at their website, review some of the courses, and write down the 3 courses they suggest that best align with your priorities from the previous page.

https://www.ecstra.org.au/financial-education-and-wellbeing

PREFERENCE	COURSE NAME	WHY IT INTERESTS ME
1		
2		
3		

Financial Services and Advice

What characteristics do you look for in someone who is giving you advice?

Learning Objective

By the end of this lesson, students will be able to:

· Describe sources of good and poor financial advice.

Key Terms

· Financial Advisor
· Bias

SOURCE OF FINANCIAL ADVICE	WHY WOULD THEY BE GOOD ADVISORS?	WHAT LIMITS OR RESERVATIONS SHOULD YOU HAVE ABOUT THEIR ADVICE? WHAT ARE THE DOWN SIDES?
Parents		
Peers		
Local Bank		
Online Financial Influencers		
Registered Financial Advisor		

Topic 29 Financial Services and Advice

Take a look at the Financial Advice Association of Australia website https://faaa.au/

Specifically read through the consumers and FAQ sections. How does this information change your perspectives on the previous page? If everyone has a bias, what is the FAAA site's bias? How does that change the way you think about seeking professional advice compared with informal advice from family and friends?

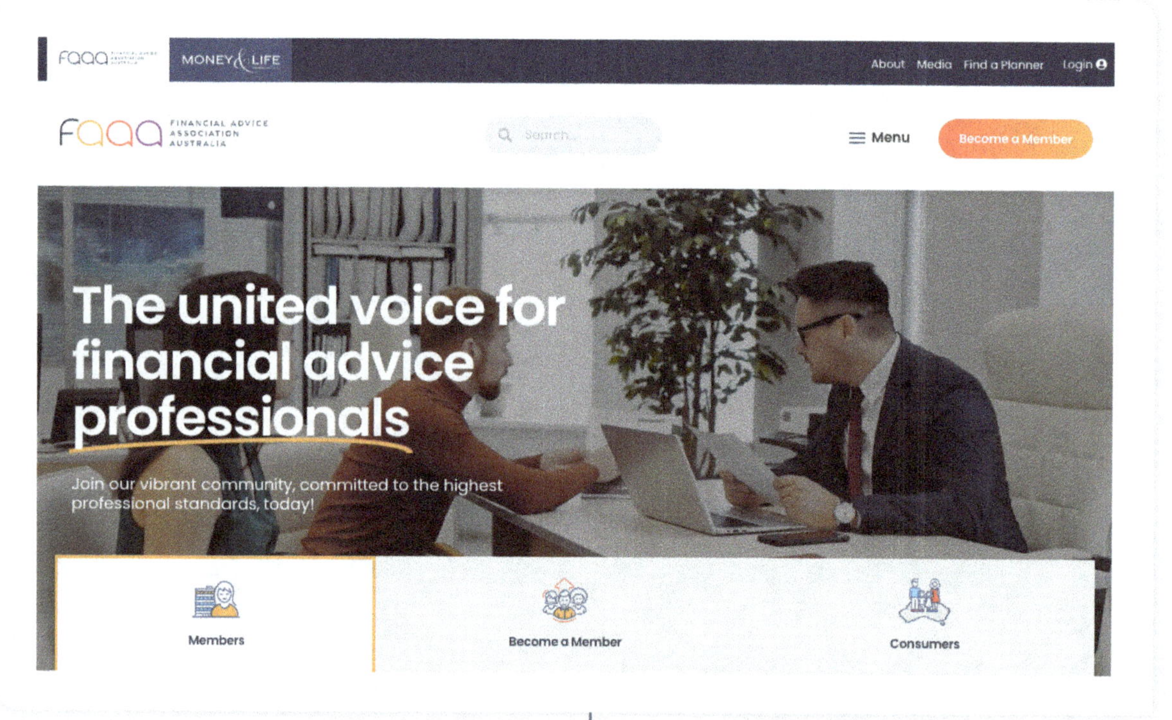

Summary Points

- Remember that advice from friends or influencers is not personal financial advice, only a licensed professional can give you tailored recommendations.

Course Post Test and Feedback

At the start of this course, you answered a series of questions to help gauge your knowledge around finance. In this topic, you will revisit the same questions with a deeper understanding and knowledge. Complete the following pages honestly and as completely as you can. After you have completed the questions, compare your answers with those in Module 1. Use 2 coloured highlighters to mark the questions you improved in most and those questions where you saw less improvement.

Learning Objective

By the end of this lesson students will be able to:

- Demonstrate growth in understanding of the financial concepts addressed in this courset.

Key Terms

- Financial Success
- Learning Growth

Topic 30 Course Post Test and Feedback

QUESTION	ANSWER
1. What is the difference between a Debit Card and a Credit Card?	
2. What is the difference between Income Tax and GST?	
3. Describe the concept of Compound Interest.	
4. What are Shares?	
5. Write a summary of what you know about Superannuation.	
6. What is a Tax File Number and who needs one?	
7. What is the difference between a casual job and a part-time job?	
8. Is renting an item or buying an item better?	
9. How might interest rates be different between a personal loan and a mortgage?	

QUESTION	ANSWER
10. What is a budget?	
11. Who spends tax income, and what do they spend it on?	
12. What is cryptocurrency?	
13. What information would you expect to see on a payslip?	
14. How is a transaction account different from a savings account?	
15. What is a credit score?	

Personal Reflection: What does financial success look like for me?

Micro-Credential Requirements

Now its time to test your new knowledge and skills. Micro credentials are a relatively new way of gaining skills and demonstrating your learning. When you go to the following link you will be taken to the Financial Success website. You should look for Topic 36 Micro Credential Exam.

https://sites.google.com/
syd.catholic.edu.au/
southern-cross-academy/
financial-success

When you go to the test, it will ask you for some basic information like your email address, name, and your current school. At the end of the test, you will be asked which of the major projects you completed. This information is important to ensure you get the certificate when you pass. The test is 50 questions long and is multiple choice throughout. You need to score 85% or better to achieve the credential.

www.ingramcontent.com/pod-product-compliance
Lightning Source LLC
Chambersburg PA
CBHW080323030726
47593CB00009B/2871